The Freshwater Angler™

FISHING

TIPS & TRICKS
More than 500 Guide-tested Tips for Freshwater and Saltwater

C. Boyd Pfeiffer

Creative Publishing
international

Minneapolis, Minnesota

C. Boyd Pfeiffer, an award-winning outdoor journalist and photographer, has been published in more than 70 magazines, including *Saltwater Fly Fishing, Outdoor Life, and American Angler.* He has authored 24 books on fishing and outdoor photography. He lives in Phoenix, Maryland.

To Brenda

Creative Publishing
international

Copyright © 2008
Creative Publishing international, Inc.
400 First Avenue North, Suite 300
Minneapolis, MN 55401
1-800-328-3895
www.creativepub.com

President/CEO: Ken Fund
VP Sales/Marketing: Kevin Hamric
Publisher: Bryan Trandem
Acquisition Editor: Barbara Harold
Production Managers: Laura Hokkanen, Linda Halls
Creative Director: Michele Lanci-Altomare
Senior Design Managers: Brad Springer, Jon Simpson
Design Managers: Sara Holle, James Kegley
Page Design & Layout: Laura Rades, LK Design, Inc.
Cover Design: Danielle Smith

All photographs © Creative Publishing international
except those © iStockPhotos on pages 32–33, and
those © C. Boyd Pfeiffer, illustrating tip numbers 3,
19, 24, 26, 31, 39, 42, 49, 54, 57, 82, 109, 140, 155,
177, 241–292, 296, 299, 303, 306, 308, 309, 313,
315, 318, 321, 322, 329, 330, 331, 335, 339, 345,
347, 349, 350, 351, 352, 357, 359, 428, 429, 430,
439, 445, 467, 485, 490.

Printed in Singapore

10 9 8 7 6 5 4 3 2 1

Library of Congress Cataloging-in-Publication Data
Pfeiffer, C. Boyd.
  Fishing tips & tricks : more than 500 guide-tested
tips & tactics for freshwater and saltwater angling /
C. Boyd Pfeiffer.
      p. cm. -- (Freshwater angler series)
ISBN-13: 978-1-58923-408-6 (hardcover)
  ISBN-10: 1-58923-408-1 (hardcover)
  1. Fishing--North America--Miscellanea. I. Title. II.
Title: Fishingtips and tricks. III. Series.

SH462.P473 2008
799.1097--dc22   2008007057

CONTENTS

INTRODUCTION

Clever fishing tips and tricks have passed from angler to angler for as long as people have fished. The Greek philosopher Aristotle once wrote that a pair of fishermen could net the skate, a flat-bodied bottom fish, if one played music while the other danced on deck.

Most fishing tips, like Aristotle's, are of questionable value. Lots of the tips you find in magazines and books have not been thoroughly tested; they may have worked for somebody, but they don't work for you. Many so-called tips are common knowledge to anybody who spends much time on the water. Others are intended simply to sell you something.

What is a good tip? Certainly, it isn't a dissertation about how to find walleyes throughout the year. That's strategy. Nor is it a description of fishing dry flies for trout. That's a tactic. Strategy and tactics are the fundamentals of good angling, but they're too comprehensive to be called tips. And a good tip isn't a sales pitch for a high-priced, high-tech gizmo. That's not a tip, it's advertising.

Rather, a good tip is a specific solution to a vexing problem. The best ones are simple and cheap. They make your fishing easier or more enjoyable. A good tip often triggers new ideas and helps you fashion your own solutions. Most important of all, a good tip helps you catch more fish.

Our challenge in writing *Fishing Tips & Tricks* was to come up with little-known bits of information of real value to freshwater and saltwater anglers. Gathering enough good tips to fill an entire book was a monumental task. We contacted thousands of the country's best guides and professional anglers. During our travels, we fished with the best anglers in every part of the country. We watched closely to spot any unique twists in their fishing methods.

After collecting thousands of morsels of advice, we sorted through them, looking for those that were new, unusual, simple, and, above all, helpful.

Then, the testing began. Our research staff spent hundreds of hours finding out if tips actually worked. If not, they experimented and tried to make the tip work. Many tips sounded good, but flopped when tested; these were eliminated. When we finished, we had more than 500 tried-and-true tips for freshwater and saltwater species found in North America. Where possible, we have given credit to the anglers who passed these tips our way. Now we pass them on to you.

This is a book you'll want to read from cover to cover. Even if you're on the water every day, you're sure to discover something in this book that will improve your fishing. In fact, you'll find some of the tips so ingenious you'll be tempted to say, "Why didn't I think of that?"

Chapter 1

GENERAL-PURPOSE TIPS

Search through this chapter to find tips that will help you in any and all fishing situations. To be sure, some tips will only apply to fishing for specific species or with use of one type of tackle, or in one particular fishing situation. Others are general and can be applied to any fishing opportunity. Check through these to find the tips that are relevant to your fishing requirements.

1

Easy Worm Container

Many grocery store products come in cans with plastic snap-on lids. Containers with these lids where you can also remove the bottom make ideal worm containers. Remove the bottom of such cans and add a snap-on lid to both top and bottom for worms. Keep the cans in a loose sphagnum moss mix. Since worms always gravitate to the bottom of any container, getting worms is easy. Just turn the container over each time and remove the lid to expose worms that were on the bottom, but are now on the top.

2

Use Split Shot on Dropper to Prevent Lure, Bait Loss

If you need weight to sink a lure or bait to the bottom, use a separate dropper on the line above the bait or lure and add a series of split shot to this dropper. Do not loop the line around the split shot or add a knot to the end of this dropper line. The spread-out weight of the split shot is less likely to cause a hang-up than would a single heavy sinker. And, if a split shot does get hung up, it is likely to pull off of the dropper line, leading to a loss of the split shot, but not the lure or baited hook.

3

Prevent Fish Injury

Bass anglers often land, unhook, and then hold bass by the lower jaw, bending the fish's jaw back to admire the fish and perhaps pose for a picture. Unfortunately, this can break or injure the jaw of the bass and make it difficult to continue eating or survive.

4

Sharpening Bait and Fillet Knives

When sharpening bait and fillet knives, it is often difficult to tell when you have the right angle with the stone and whether or not the blades are getting sharp. An easy way to check this is to use a fat, ¼-inch-wide (6 mm) black felt-tip marker, drawn along the edge of both sides of the blade. Proper sharpening removes the black mark on the blade. If the black mark is still there after sharpening, the correct blade or hone angle was not used or you have missed a spot.

5

Gaff Alternative

Nets cause less damage to a fish than a gaff, even if gaffing in the lip to release a fish. Use a net with rubber mesh, which also is less likely to tangle or catch lure hooks than a nylon-knotted or woven net. It also does less damage to the fish if you plan on release. After netting and removing the hook, it is easy to turn the net over to release the fish.

6

Eat High-Energy Foods When Winter Fishing

To keep your strength and energy up when winter fishing, eat high-energy and high-calorie food and snacks.

7

Bring the Worms to You

To attract worms and keep them in a spot where they are easily gathered, make a worm bed. Place several inches of matted straw over dirt you have loosened and turned with a garden fork. Keep the straw moist to draw worms.

A better way to hold a bass is so it hangs straight down. Or, support the belly and body when holding it at an angle or sideways.

8

Long Live the Leeches

To ensure you always have leeches on hand, buy several pounds in the spring when they're plentiful and cheap. Leeches can be kept alive for months in a refrigerator. Take out only as many as you need on your fishing trip. Most of the leeches you don't use will survive a day on the water and can be returned to the fridge. But keep them separate from leeches in long-term storage. Putting dead or dying leeches in with healthy ones may kill them all. The photos show how to keep your leeches in good shape.

9

Striking with Circle Hooks

To strike a fish when using a circle hook, don't actually strike. Unlike standard "J" hooks that you must strike with bait or a lure to ensure the fish is hooked, circle hooks work differently. Circle hooks have a sharply bent-in point (like the claw of a predatory bird). When fishing bait, allow the fish to take the bait and start to run with it. Even if the fish has swallowed the bait, the hook usually slides until catching in the corner of the fish's mouth. The same thing happens with fishing lures equipped with circle hooks. The advantage of these hooks is that they are very sure hookers once you are used to fishing with them. They also allow catch-and-release without deep-hooking and harming the fish.

10

No More Messy Worms

Digging through a pail full of worms and bedding makes a mess of your boat, hands, and clothes. Instead, drop several dozen worms in a bucket of ice. Meltwater cleans the worms and they'll survive all day. When you're done fishing, put the worms back into the bedding. If they crawl down, they're still healthy.

11

Avoid Bobber Stop Hang-Ups

The advantage of a slip-bobber over a regular bobber is that you can cast it easily, even when you're fishing deep. But the bobber stop can interfere with casting. If it happens to wind onto the front edge of your spool, it can catch outgoing line, causing your cast to fall short or to stop suddenly and snap off the bait.

1. Store leeches in a polyfoam bucket in a refrigerator; the water should be barely above freezing—34 to 38°F (1 to 3°C). Change water every few days to keep it clean. Store an extra container of water in the refrigerator. When you change water, the fresh water will be at the same temperature and any chlorine will be gone.

2. Add a few ice cubes to your bait bucket as you fish to keep the water cool. If the water is allowed to get warm, leeches begin to mature and spawn. The process begins at about 50°F (10°C) and accelerates as the temperature rises. Once leeches mature, they die within several days, even if you return them to cold water.

12

Fishing a Worm Beneath a Bobber

If you're fishing a nightcrawler with a slip-sinker, hook it once through the head so it trails behind the hook. But don't hook it this way when you bobber-fish because the worm dangles vertically. You'll miss strikes and fish will steal your bait. The photo shows a better way to hook your worm when bobber fishing.

13

Keep Crawlers Lively

Worms kept in something other than a thick Styrofoam container get limp and lifeless on a warm day. If they get too hot, they'll die. Here's a way to keep worms lively, even in the hottest weather.

Put a few ice cubes in a small resealable plastic bag and bury it in the bedding. The worms stay cool for hours. Without the bag, the melting ice cubes would make the bedding too soggy.

14

Bagging Weights for Disposable Sinkers

If fishing an area where sinkers are known to get snagged and lost, use scrap metal on a light line that will break off if snagged. Some scrap metal, such as spark plugs, are easy to tie to a light line, tying to the metal contacts. Other scrap metal can also be used, secured in a bag made of an old nylon stocking. Use a square of stocking material, add the metal, and tie the nylon bag with light line to add to a bottom fishing rig. Scrap for these disposable sinkers can be old nuts and bolts, tire wheel weights, or any other metal. Be sure not to use lead weights in areas where it is prohibited for fishing.

15

Depth-Mark Anchor Rope

It is good to know how much anchor line is out for both checking the depth of the water as well as determining the anchor rode (or length of line) to safely get an anchor to hold. Anchor rode varies with weather conditions and bottom type—check with a seamanship book for suggestions. Mark your anchor line with a band using a black felt tip marker or black electricians tape. Mark it every 10 feet (3 m), using one band for 10 feet, two bands for 20 feet (6 m), three bands for 30 feet (9 m), etc. When reaching 50 feet (15 m), use a wide band. Continue with one wide band and one narrow band for 60 feet (18 m) and so on.

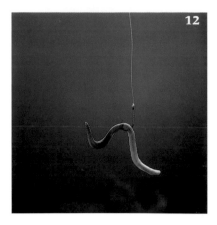

Hook the worm twice through the middle when suspending it below a bobber. This way, you're more likely to hook a fish that doesn't suck in the entire worm.

16

Nightcrawler Substitute

If it's been too dry to collect nightcrawlers or if you can't find them at your local bait shop, it's tough to find a good substitute. The photo shows a trick that may salvage your fishing trip.

17

Diagnose Fly-Casting Faults

A good forward cast is easy for most fly-fishermen because they can watch the fly line and correct their casting faults. The problem is the backcast: it's tough to glance backward over your shoulder to make adjustments to your casting stroke. For that reason, many fishermen have lousy backcasts and cast poorly overall.

If you have trouble with your backcast, such as hitting the water or ground behind you with the line, use my trick to study your problem and correct it.

18

Trigger Strikes While Trolling

When you're trolling with plugs, spinners, or spoons, drop your rod tip back once in a while rather than maintaining a steady pull. Dropping back causes the lure to tumble momentarily, triggering strikes from any fish that may be following.

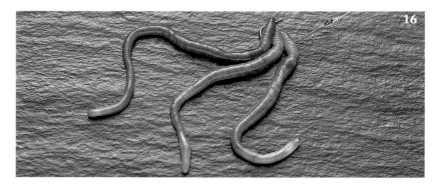

String three garden worms on a single hook. Push about ¼ inch (6 mm) of the head of each worm onto the hook and let the tails wiggle freely. The squirming worms work as well as, and sometimes even better than, a crawler.

1. Stand sideways to your target (a Hula Hoop makes a good one) with your feet spread comfortably, like a batter standing at the plate. Lower your rod so it is parallel to the ground and cast sidearm rather than overhand.

2. Watch the fly line as you make your backcast and forward cast. Adjust your timing and casting stroke until the line unfurls smoothly, forming narrow loops forward and backward.

3. Turn back toward your target and cast with an overhand motion instead of sidearm. The timing and motion remain nearly identical, even though the casting plane changes from horizontal to vertical.

19

Quick-Fix Big Sinkers

One way to quickly make a large sinker into a better holding sinker for tough conditions is to place a bank sinker in a vise and hammer nails into the perimeter of the large lead body. You can also do the same with a pyramid sinker, hammering nails into four flat sides on the upper part of the sinker. The resulting sinkers grip the bottom better and have less of a tendency to roll with current, tide, or surf-fishing wave action.

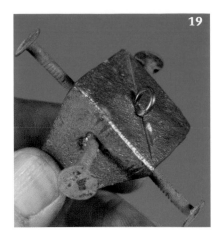

20

"Easy Pickings" for Crawlers

Because crawlers are so expensive, lots of anglers try to collect their own, but most are lucky to get enough for a day's fishing.

Here's how you can catch enough nightcrawlers in just an hour or two to last most of the season. All you need is an underground worm bed or an old refrigerator to keep them in.

- Most worm pickers go out at night, but you can often find more worms in early morning, especially if it has been drizzling all night. By morning, the worms are crawling some distance from their burrows, so catching them is easy. And you don't need a light. The best early-morning spots are golf course greens and the gutters along paved streets.
- Some golf courses produce lots of crawlers; others, very few. The trick is to find the ones that don't apply chemicals to control the worms.
- Check well-established lawns. A newly seeded or sodded lawn may not produce crawlers for several years and if the soil is too sandy or gravelly, it may never produce.
- Look for crawlers during or after a prolonged light rain or drizzle. Worms don't like being pelted by heavy rain. The air temperature should be at least 50°F (10°C). Otherwise, worms stay in the ground.
- Wait until a couple of hours after dark so the nightcrawlers are out of their burrows. If their tails are still anchored, the worms zip back in when they detect a light or feel the vibrations from your footsteps.
- Cover your flashlight lens with red cellophane. This way, the light doesn't seem to bother the worms. Step lightly to keep vibrations to a minimum.
- Pick up crawlers on a paved street using a spatula. It's difficult to get your fingers under the wet, slippery worms.

21

Unwrap Line Quickly

It's happened to nearly every angler: when you're fishing, you notice a wrap of line around your rod. You're not sure how the wrap got there, but it seems the only way to get rid of it is to restring your rod. There's an easier way.

22

Fishing Deep with a Sinker in Front of a Diving Crankbait

Sometimes the only way to get deep is with an in-line sinker in front of a crankbait. To do this without ruining the action of the crankbait, tie the in-line sinker to the end of the line and then tie a 2- to 3-foot (60 to 90 cm) length of line to the other sinker eye and then to the line tie on the lure. The added length of the line between the sinker and lure will help prevent any deadening of lure action.

23

When to Use Weaker Line on Dropper

When fishing deep with weight on a dropper line, use a thinner and weaker line for the dropper. That way, if the sinker that is dragging the bait or lure across the bottom gets caught, it is easy to break the line and lose the sinker while not losing the more expensive hook, bait, or lure.

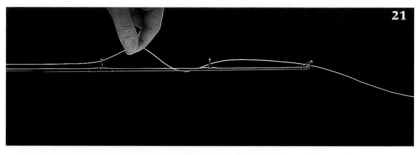

1. Grab the line where it wraps around the rod between two of the guides.

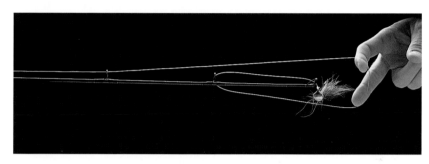

2. Pull the line over the tiptop or butt of the rod, whichever is easier.

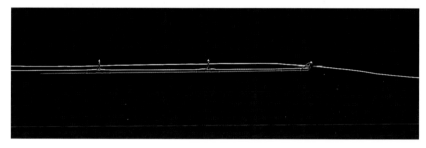

3. Release the line and the line runs from guide to guide without the once-around wrap.

24

Store Reels on Perf Board Rack

One easy way to store lots of reels is on a perf board rack using the perf board hooks.

For spinning reels, use 1-inch (2.5 cm) curved hooks to hold the reel foot on both sides of the reel arm.

For casting reels, use two small curved hooks to hold the reel by the cross bars that connect the right and left side plates.

For fly reels, use one straight hook to hold the reel by one of the crossbars connecting the frame parts.

This makes it easy to see the reels at all times and to aid in picking the best tackle for any fishing trip.

25

No-Tangle Throw Rope

A long rope can save the life of someone who has fallen overboard and is struggling in the water. But it takes too long to untangle a rope that lies in a heap in the bottom of the boat.

Here's a system of rigging a long throw rope so it can be thrown immediately and accurately. It's handy not only in boating accidents, but in ice-fishing mishaps as well.

Make a throw rope (top) by punching a ⅜-inch (1 cm) hole in the bottom of a plastic jug. Thread 50 feet (15 m) of ⅜-inch (1 cm) rope through the bottom hole and out the top. Tie a loop at each end. Pull one knot snug against the outside bottom of the jug. Feed the rest of the rope into the mouth of the bottle. Toss the rope to a victim by holding the loop at the mouth of the jug, grabbing the jug by the handle, and throwing it underhand (bottom). The rope will peel out smoothly from the mouth as the jug sails through the air. The victim can get a firm hold of the loop at the jug end.

26

Pipe Insulation Makes Great Rod Carrier, Protection

Fly rods, casting rods, and tip sections of spinning rods are easily protected by slipping them into a length of foam pipe insulation. This is good protection in a car or in a boat. Buy pipe insulation with the largest diameter hole for maximum use. Most pipe insulation comes in packs of four 3-foot (1 m) lengths. To adjust the pipe insulation, seal the split-open side with contact cement, such as Pliobond. You can also glue two lengths together and cut as desired to make custom lengths. Taping with duct tape also works.

27

Use Oatmeal to Catch Baitfish

Oatmeal is ideal for attracting and catching baitfish. To do this, first spread out a square dip net (available commercially) on the bottom of a small creek or close to the shore of a pond. Wait a few minutes and then scatter some oatmeal on the surface. When baitfish come for the oatmeal, jerk the net out of the water to capture the bait. Make sure you have a bait bucket filled with water into which you can dump the baitfish. Also make sure it is legal to capture bait this way or in the area where you are doing it. In some states, it is not legal on trout streams.

28

Use Round Sinkers when Saltwater Wreck Fishing

Bank and pyramid sinkers or other styles of slim sinkers easily get hung up on rocky bottoms and especially in the saltwater wrecks fished for tautog, sea bass, and tilefish. To reduce the possibility of losing sinkers, use round cannonball sinkers instead. They are less likely than bank sinkers to drop into small holes in wrecks and get hung up.

29

Store Pack Rods in PVC Tubing

An easy way to home-store three- and four-piece pack rods is to keep them in a cloth rod bag and store them in 2-foot-long (60 cm) vertical rod racks made of 4-inch (10 cm) PVC drain pipe. Cut the drain pipe to length and then cut a round wood "cap" to fit into the cut end, held in place with screws or nails. If you have many rods, store each line-size rod in a separate tube and mark the outside of the tube with the size of the rod it holds.

30

Prevent Line Twist

When you're jigging vertically, whether in open water or through the ice, the lure usually spins around and causes severe line twist. The twisted line tends to wrap around your rod tip and tangle in your guides. To prevent the problem, tie a small swivel to your line, a foot or two (30 to 60 cm) above the lure.

31

Foam Float Rod Helps Dry Waders

To dry out waders, fold them down and place them outside on a sunny day. To keep the waders or hip boots open for rapid drying, fill the waders with a loose bundle of newspapers or with sections of rod-like foam floats.

32

Adjust Drag While Fighting Fish

Some anglers suggest setting a drag and not changing it at all while fishing. This works fine if the fish is not big or only makes short runs, but it can lead to a lost fish. If fighting a big, long-running fish, realize that as line is taken by the fish, the effective spool diameter of the reel grows smaller, leverage on the reel changes, and the drag becomes heavier. To adjust for this, set the drag for striking and fighting a fish, but be prepared to loosen it to prevent break-offs if the fish makes a long run. As you gain line in fighting the fish, slightly tighten the drag again to the preset position.

   When landing a big fish, it also helps to slightly loosen the drag. This is because there is little shock-absorbing line out and a sudden burst of speed can cause the line to break. In all of this, make sure that you never exceed the drag originally set on the reel for that line test. Reels that have lever drags or some way to mark the drag for reference are best for this.

33

How to Get Lures Deep

Fish deep by using light line, fishing slowly, making long casts, and using deep-diving lures. By using deep-diving lures, you maximize the possible depth. Light lines have less water resistance than heavier lines and thus also allow deeper fishing. Slow retrieves also allow a lure to get to its maximum depth. Long casts, with the rod held low on retrieve, also keep the lure deep in the strike zone longer.

34

Heading off a Bird's Nest

If you're using a spinning reel and retrieve without much tension on the line, a loop of mono will often form at the front of the spool and interfere with the outgoing line as you cast. If you try to peel off line to get rid of the loop, the loop will also begin to peel off and tangle with the other line, often forming a snarl several feet (m) long. It may be impossible to untangle the line without cutting it.

There is a good way to head off a tangle before it occurs and save precious fishing time.

35

Keep the Float Worm Visible

Fish such as bass feed on the bottom, but if they cannot find your worm, they can't hit it. One way to solve this is to use a light jig with a floating worm so the jig sinks, but the worm floats above the bottom. You can use an exposed hook rig by gluing (CA glue) the worm to the hook shank or using a stinger hook with the eye buried in the worm and impaled by the jig hook.

36

Save Bug Dope for Bugs

If you get insect repellent containing DEET on your hands, it can soften vinyl fly line coatings, weaken monofilament line, damage lure finishes, eat away at line spools, dissolve non-wormproof tackle boxes, and damage the screens of liquid crystal recorders. Here's a way to avoid the problem:

Apply the bug dope first to the backs of your hands. Then use the backs of your hands to spread the repellent to your face, neck, and arms. This is a good tip for the camp cook as well, so the repellent doesn't get in the food.

Sunscreen can also have chemicals that are repellent to fish, so use the same "back of the hands" technique for adding sunscreen to exposed skin before fishing.

37

Water-Stored Spool Prevents Coils

To soften monofilament spinning line and make it more flexible for fishing, remove the spool from the reel and place it in a zipper-lock bag with a little water. Do this a day or two before fishing so the water has time to be absorbed into the line to reduce tight coiling.

Open the bail and remove the spool when you notice that a loop has formed. Because these loops form at the front of the spool, it's best to pull line off the back of the spool to avoid tangling the outgoing line with the loop. After you pull off the loop, replace the spool, close the bail, and reel in the loose line.

Bobber Helps You Get Unsnagged

River rats know that if you snag your lure downstream, you may be able to pull free by letting out enough line to form a belly several yards below the snag. When you give a sharp tug, water resistance against the line produces a downstream pull that may free the lure. But if the lure is tightly snagged, this technique won't work. The photo shows a way to produce a stronger downstream pull and free the lure.

Add Weight Designation to Sinkers

If heavy saltwater sinkers do not have the weight in ounces molded into the side or if the number has worn off, you can easily add the weight designation using a regular screwdriver. For this, weigh each sinker on a postage or package scale and mark it with the screw driver. The system of using a screwdriver is to mark the sinker using a Roman numbering system, lightly hitting the screwdriver into the side of the sinker to make a straight line. Thus, you can mark any weight in ounces, using a "I" for 1 through 4, two strikes to make a "V" for 5 and crossed strikes "X" to make a 10. Thus, a sinker marked with a VIII is 8 ounces, a XII for a 12-ounce sinker, and IIII for a 4-ounce sinker.

You can use the same system with small (under 1 ounce, 128g) sinkers by using a small regular screwdriver to mark the weight in $\frac{1}{16}$-ounce fractions (1.7g). Thus a sinker marked III would be $\frac{3}{16}$ (5.3g), one marked VIII would be $\frac{8}{16}$ or $\frac{1}{2}$ ounce (14g), etc.

Chum in a Paper Bag

To get chum deep, do not just throw it over the side of the boat. It dissipates too much or small fish get it before the big fish on the bottom even know that it is there. Instead, add chum to a paper bag. Add a few stones to weight the bag. Then tie the mouth of the bag with string and tie your fishing line to the wrapped string. Use a stout rod for this chum placement. Carefully lower the bag over the side where you wish to fish and lower the weighed chum bag to the bottom. Wait a few minutes for the water to soak the bag and then jerk your rod briskly to tear the bag free of the chum, distribute the chum, and retrieve the bag for proper disposal. Wait a few minutes for the chum to disperse and then start fishing bait or jigging the bottom.

Clip a big bobber to the eye of a snap-swivel. Close the snap over your line. Open your bail and let the current carry the bobber well past the snag. Close your bail. When the line tightens, give a sharp tug. The added resistance of the bobber results in a stronger downstream pull than that produced by the line alone. Other floats, such as plastic bottles, also work and these can be partially filled with water to increase the drag and the power of your pull.

41

Wash Reels After Each Saltwater Fishing Trip

Some experts disagree about the best way to wash off a reel after a day of saltwater fishing. All agree that you should never use a hose on a reel, since this can force salt spray and residue into the reel through joints and crevices. Some anglers like to thoroughly coat a reel with a demoisturizer such as WD-40 before fishing, then just gently wash down the reel with a rag soaked in warm freshwater after each trip. Others like to soak a reel for a few minutes in a freshwater bath, then dry it thoroughly and recoat with a demoisturizer.

42

Tackle Emergency Kit

An emergency kit to care for tackle is always a good idea and particularly so on long or several-day trips where a tackle shop might be far away. Some basics for a kit like this include:
- Spare guides in several sizes and types
- Tip tops in several tube diameters for quick repairs
- Heat-set cement (ferrule cement) to quickly glue on tip tops
- Tape to temporarily secure guides to a rod
- Reel grease and oil—small tubes
- Line clippers (nail clippers)
- Spare hooks (single and treble) for bait and lures
- Split ring pliers (for adding new hooks)
- Safety pin for removing glue, paint from the eyes of hooks, flies, and lures
- Set of small screwdrivers for tightening screws in reels

Fly fishermen also want fly line cleaner, wax for rod ferrules, fly floatant and sink.

Carry such a kit in a small six-compartment lure box, a zippered pencil case, or small waterproof case as is sold in many outdoor stores.

42

43

Fly Fishing in the Wind

Wind gives fly fishermen fits. You can't drive your forward cast into the wind and a wind at your back causes the backcast to pile up, which means the forward cast is no good either. But wind doesn't have to ruin your fly fishing. The photo shows how to make good casts, either into the wind or with it.

1. Casting into the Wind. Cast sidearm, keeping your forward cast as low to the water as possible. This way, the wind has little effect on it. Loft your backcast a bit (dotted line) so the wind helps straighten it out.

44

More Accurate Spinning

One problem with open-face spinning: it isn't as accurate at short distances as baitcasting. The baitcaster can lightly thumb the spool to control the cast or press down to stop the plug and make it land in just the right spot.

But once an angler casts a spinning outfit, it's tough to stop the lure on target—unless you use this trick.

Slide your hand back on the handle far enough so you can pinch the line against the spool with your index finger. Flip the bail and cast, releasing line by moving your finger. You can slow the lure down by feathering the line with your index finger or press the spool to end the cast. This trick works only with small and medium-sized reels; big reels are mounted too far off the rod to reach with your finger.

2. Casting with the Wind. Cast sidearm, keeping your backcast low and shorter than normal. Aim higher with the forward cast (dotted line) so the wind catches it, adding to your distance.

45

Follow Birds to Fish

Birds can lead you to good ice-fishing spots. If there are no anglers or fish houses on a lake to give away the location of a hotspot, you can often pinpoint the site of recent fishing activity by watching birds, such as crows or gulls, which often congregate where anglers have discarded bait or small fish.

During the open-water season, look for loons, cormorants, or fish-eating ducks diving in off-shore areas. The birds are feeding on small fish, which are probably relating to a reef or some kind of cover. Gamefish are likely to be there along with them.

46

Finer Fiddle for Worms

Southeastern anglers collect grunt worms by "fiddling"—rubbing an ax head or piece of steel on a wooden stake driven into the ground. The vibrations draw worms to the surface. Here's a way to make a stake that produces stronger vibrations with less effort and will help you get more worms.

Cut ¼-inch-deep (6 mm) saw kerfs at ½-inch (13 mm) intervals along one side of a 2 x 2-inch (5 x 5 cm) stake about 30 inches (76 cm) long. Make a point on one end and drive the stake about a foot into the ground.

Rub another stick, such as a piece of broom handle, rapidly up and down across the saw cuts.

47

Use Dual Bait Drag/Conventional Reel Drag for Surf Fishing

Spinning reels by some manufacturers, such as Okuma, Zebco, and Shimano, have two drag systems. One is a traditional front drag designed to fight the fish. The second is a very light rear drag with a quick lever "off" switch to remove all drag and switch the reel to the front drag. Use these for bait fishing in the surf. To use properly, set the front drag for fighting the fish, using a drag appropriate to the line test used. Set the rear drag lightly so line does not flow off of the reel, but so the fish can take line against the light drag without feeling the heavy front drag that would cause the fish to drop the bait. This prevents outfits from being pulled out of sand spikes and into the sand and allows letting a fish run until ready to switch off of the rear drag and set the hook to fight the fish with the front drag.

48

Acclimate Minnows

Most minnows are sensitive to rapid changes in water temperature. Always keep this in mind when handling your bait.

Many anglers believe they can keep their minnows alive on a hot day by adding ice. But they're often surprised to find all the minnows dead within minutes. Icing your minnows can help, but don't add too much ice at once. If you lower the temperature of the water by more than about 10°F (5.5°C) at a time, the minnows often die from temperature shock.

You can also kill minnows by moving them from cool water to warm. This problem occurs most frequently when anglers transfer minnows in a cool oxygen pack to the warm water of a cooler, bait well, or flow-through minnow bucket. The photo shows how to solve the problem.

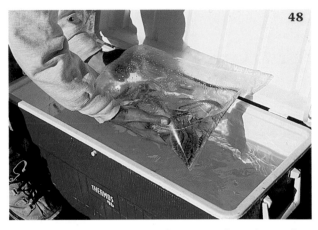

Place the unopened oxygen pack into a cooler or bait well to slowly warm the water inside the bag and acclimate the minnows to the change in temperature. After about a half-hour, the water in the pack will be the same temperature and you can open the bag.

49

Line Tips for Winter Fishing

Line conditioners keep lines pliable for fishing without any harmful effects. Another good line tip for winter fishing is to use braided or fluorocarbon lines that are more expensive but not affected by cold water. Nylon monofilament line absorbs water and under extremely cold conditions will freeze, making the line stiff. Braided lines stay flexible and fluorocarbon lines do not absorb water.

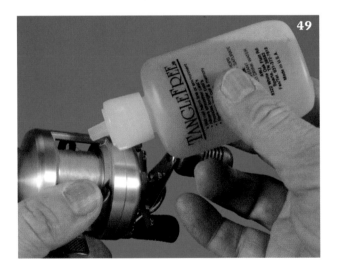

50

Don't Overlook Docks

Fishing docks is a good strategy after a cold front passes. Bass that were holding around the edges of the dock before the front tuck up into the thickest cover and deepest shade under the dock. Skip a plastic worm or jig as far back under the dock as possible and retrieve very slowly. Also try fishing boat hoists next to docks; the underwater struts and posts provide security for inactive fish.

51

Use Safety Strips on Trailer "Walk Boards"

Many small boat trailers have a "walk board" by which you can walk down the length of the trailer to attach the winch rope when retrieving a boat. To make these even safer, add safety strips to prevent slipping. These are available in most hardware and home supply stores. Make sure you add these self-stick strips when the walk board is completely dry.

Fight Fish Smart

If you hook a large, powerful fish with normal-weight tackle, you may not be able to wear it down by lifting with steady tension. The fish can resist without moving much and doesn't get tired. Here are a couple ways to tire big fish quickly and increase your odds of landing them.

Work a fish in shallow water by pulling it to one side, switching the rod to the other side, and pulling from the opposite direction. Pulling from the side with the rod tip low to the water forces the fish to struggle to regain its balance, so it tires quickly. The closer the fish is, the more effectively you can use the rod to wear it down.

If a large fish is sulking underneath the boat, work it with short, quick pumps of the rod, taking in just a few inches (cm) of line each time. Those quick tugs get a fish off the bottom and moving in your direction better than either a steady pull or a long, slow pumping motion.

Use Weak Line with Disposable Sinker in Trolling Rig

Very deep trolling often requires larger sinkers or weight that impedes the fight of the fish. To have the fun without the sinker weight, use old metal "junk" to make up trolling weights. Tie these items to a short length of line and form a loop knot in the end of the line. Then tie two in-line loop knots in your main fishing line, with these two knots about 1 to 2 feet (30 to 60 cm) apart. Tie a much lighter line between the two loops so the main line is slack between these two loops. Run this lighter line through the sinker/weight loop before tying to the second line loop. When a fish hits, the impact causes the light line to break, releasing the weight/sinker and allowing you to fight the fish without any resistance.

54

Store Rods in Overhead Loops and Hooks

If you have a lot of different rods, one easy way to store them is with overhead racks fastened to the basement rafters.

55

Ice Fishing Safety

Unfortunately, some of the year's best ice fishing occurs when the ice is most dangerous: right after freeze-up and just before ice-out. Unless you're sure the ice is safe, stay off it, no matter how well the fish are biting.

River ice can be especially treacherous. The current weakens it and keeps it from freezing uniformly. Any time you're ice fishing early or late in the season or on a river, take extra precautions. Test the ice thickness with a sharp ice chisel and carry an ice pick so you can pull yourself out if you do fall through. Here are a couple of other tips for crossing ice safely.

Carry a long stick or sapling. If you fall in, the stick will bridge the hole and provide support so you can lift yourself onto solid ice. If a friend falls through, you can crawl over the ice, pushing the stick in front of you to reach him and help pull him to safety.

Wear a life vest under your coat. If you break through, the vest will keep you afloat and conserve body heat. A good alternative is a "float coat," which looks like a regular parka but has built-in flotation.

56

Cleaning Worms Before Fishing

One way to condition worms for fishing is to remove them from their worm bedding a few days before fishing and place them temporarily in a bed of coffee grounds. The coffee grounds clean the dirt through the worms so they are ready to fish without the mess. Once finished fishing, place any unused worms back in their standard bedding until the next fishing trip.

1. Make up two lathing strips—one with 1-inch (2.5 cm) hooks in it 2 inches (5 cm) apart, the other with nylon strap loops 6 inches (15 cm) long placed 2 inches (5 cm) apart. Then place the two lathing strips in the rafters, parallel, but about 3 feet (0.9 m) apart. To use, slip a rod handle into the loop end of the hanger and then cradle the blank in the cup hook end.

2. You can leave rods assembled rather than breaking them down into their several pieces. You can even leave reels on the rod, but make sure that you have the loop or hook support near the reel to prevent undo strain on the rod blank.

57

Ballpoint Pen Tip Protects Spinnerbaits from Weeds

Weeds can get caught in the knot and tag end of line tied to a spinnerbait. Spinnerbaits are often fished through algae and weeds, so this can be a constant problem. To lessen snags, cut off the end of used ballpoint pens and use this small cone as a weed protector. Weeds tend to slide off these cones to make each cast with the lure more effective and more likely to get a hit.

58

Avoid a Gummy Mess

Soft-plastic lures react with many other items in your tackle box, bonding the materials together and bleeding the colors. The warmer the weather, the faster the reaction takes place.

All soft-plastic lures are made of polyvinyl chloride, the same plastic that makes up a rigid PVC pipe. The lures are softer than the pipe because they contain more petroleum-based "plasticizer." The plasticizer oozes to the surface of the lure and dissolves such things as plastic hook boxes, tackle boxes that aren't "wormproof," paint on many lures, and "living rubber" spinnerbait skirts and jig dressings.

Take plastic grubs off spinnerbaits at the end of the day. Sort all soft plastics by color and store them in separate wormproof compartments or in plastic bags.

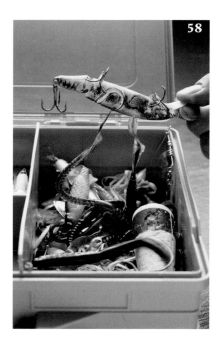

59

Packing Tackle for Travel

To pack tackle for airline travel, it must go in your checked bags. Wrap reels in underwear to protect them from damage. Keep all lures in storage boxes and seal with tape or rubber bands to prevent loose lures. Store items such as hand gaffs, pliers, dehookers, and bait and fillet knives sheathed and protected in a large plastic bag. Place a note on the top of all clothing that the travel bag contains fishing tackle, so as to alert those TSA agents making baggage hand-checks. Pack rods are best stored in short, durable multi-rod cases. Standard length rods are best in long multi-rod cases.

60

Handy Minnow Storage

Ice fishermen often end the day with a good supply of healthy minnows. Rather than carry them home or throw them away, you can keep them beneath the ice at your fish house, so they stay healthy for days and are easy to retrieve on your next fishing trip.

61

Marinade Soft Lures in Scent

To make soft plastic lures more attractive to fish, marinade them first in a scent or attractant. To do this, place soft plastic lures in a plastic zipper-lock bag along with your favorite scent or liquid attractant. Allow to marinade for several hours or overnight before fishing. That way, your soft plastics are already soaked in scent when you go to fish. Since there are many different formulas of soft plastics and also of attractants, try this first with a few baits to make sure there is no adverse chemical reaction.

62

Another Fiddler Tip

Use a pitchfork (the kind with heavy tines—not a light hay fork) to make worm fiddler. Stick it straight into the ground and, if necessary, stand on the crosspiece to get the tines into the dirt several inches more. Then "twang" the handle—pulling on it and then letting go. Do this several times to set up vibrations as the fork vibrates back and forth. This will bring up worms from around the area. When you have exhausted the area, move to another spot on the lawn and try again for more worms.

63

Harden Saltwater Baits in Sun

To help keep saltwater baits on the hook, harden them with a little time in the sun. This works well for baits such as squid, clams, oysters, cut crab, mussels, etc. It is not necessary for shrimp, most cut bait, conch, or similar baits. The hardening process in the sun helps to toughen the bait to stay on the hook and reduces bait stealing by crabs and small fish.

1. Pour the minnows into a perforated can attached to a 6-foot (1.8 m) rope with a stick tied to the other end. Lower the can down a hole drilled just outside the house, as close as possible to the fishing hole inside the house. Let the rope freeze into the ice.

2. Retrieve the minnows by sliding a long hook made from a coat hanger down your ice-fishing hole. Snag the cord, hoist the can into the fish house, and pour the minnows into your bait bucket. When you're done for the day, sink the minnows back down the fishing hole.

64

Sea Anchor Savvy

Anglers on big water commonly use sea anchors to reduce their drifting or trolling speed. But sea anchors have many other boat-control applications.

65

Carry Extra Terminal Tackle on Tape

One easy way to carry a few extra terminal tackle items with you on a short fishing trip is to secure those items between two layers of tape. You can use any type of tape including transparent paper tape, electricians tape, and masking tape. The best tape is the colored painters tape that easily comes apart and leaves no residue on terminal tackle items.

66

Cut a Backlash Short

Even expert baitcasters get backlashes, especially when they're casting into the wind. The phot shows a trick that minimizes the amount of line involved in a bird's nest and keeps you from ruining all the line on your spool.

67

Easy Line-Metering Method

A troller needs to know how much line is trailing behind the boat. Here's an easy way to gauge the amount of line you let out: Count the number of times the levelwind travels back and forth as you let out line. Try different amounts of line until you start catching fish. You can easily return to the productive depth by letting out the same number of passes.

68

Use Attractants in Winter for Slow-Moving Fish

Fish metabolism slows as much as 50 percent for each 18°F (10°C) drop in temperature. Thus, cold-weather and winter fishing is often for fish that are moving slowly and eating less than they do in the summer. To catch fish in the winter, consider bait fishing. If using lures, try slow-moving lures that can soak up attractants. Worms and jigs are better than crankbaits and spoons.

Backtroll with the wind by extending a sea anchor from your bow and running your motor in reverse. Without a sea anchor, the wind would swing your bow around, making precise boat control impossible. The sea anchor has enough drag to prevent the bow from switching around in the wind, so you can easily follow the bottom contour.

Lay a piece of plastic tape across the spool after stripping out a bit more line than you're likely to cast. Reel the line over the tape. Now, even if you get a backlash, the tangle will go no deeper than the tape. If you have to cut the line to clear the spool, you'll still have plenty left.

69

De-icing Your Auger

After cutting a hole in the ice, most fishermen set their auger down in the snow. But snow sticks to the wet blades, turns to slush, and freezes solid within minutes. Once frozen, the ice is difficult to get off, and if too much builds up on the blades and threads of the auger, the tool won't cut. There's a simple way to keep your hand or power auger ice-free.

70

Loosen Drag on Reels After Each Trip

Drags on fishing reels are made up of a series of soft and hard washers. The "soft" washers are made of graphite, leather, durable plastics, and similar materials. Hard washers are alternatively keyed to the shaft and the spool. This is best typically seen on drags of spinning reels. To prevent the soft washers from deforming in time and making the reel erratic, be sure to back off—loosen—the drag after each fishing day. Be sure to reset the drag before fishing the next day.

71

Casting in the Wind

When using spinning or casting tackle in windy situations, use the wind to your advantage or at least don't make it a disadvantage. If casting with the wind behind you, make a high arcing cast so the wind carries the line and lure for a long distance and maximum retrieve coverage. If casting against the wind, make a low, hard cast (easier with spinning than casting tackle) to throw the line and lure under the wind and to get the maximum distance. If the wind is from the side, angle the cast into the wind side to minimize any blowback and to put the lure or bait near the target.

Knock the ice off the auger with a small hammer you carry in your ice-fishing gear. Be careful not to nick the cutting edge with the hammer.

72

Old Toothbrush Makes Hook Disgorger

Make a hook disgorger for panfish and other small species by cutting the brush off an old toothbrush handle and cutting a "V" into one end. You can cut this notch with a file or with a hacksaw blade. Use this by inserting the disgorger into the mouth of the hooked fish, push the "V" notch against the bend of the hook, and push back to remove the hook point from the fish.

73

Make Travel Rod Case from PVC Pipe

It is safer and easier to carry rods in a large travel case when on a trip. To make such a case, use a 4-inch-diameter (10 cm) section of PVC pipe, either the thin-walled drain pipe or a heavier schedule-40 pipe for airline travel. Close one end permanently, using an end cap glued on with PVC glue or a round section of shelving board cut to fit inside of the pipe. Use a slip-on or screw-on cap for the opening end. Keep each rod in a flannel or carry bag to protect it from contact with other rods. Such cases can be made any length; if carrying two-piece rods, a case no more than 5 feet (1.5 m) long is best.

74

Easy-to-See Ice Fishing Line

The light, clear monofilament used when ice fishing for panfish is difficult to see. You can't tell when your lure is on the bottom and you can't see the line on the ice. Solve the problem by spooling up with 4-pound-test (1.8 kg) fluorescent yellow monofilament, which is easy to see. Use a 3-foot (0.9 m) leader of clear mono, which is nearly invisible to the fish.

75

Drift into Breaking Fish

When saltwater fishing, breaking fish signal a great opportunity to take fish on light spinning, casting, and fly tackle. To keep from driving these fish away or down deep, do not run your boat through the school. For best results, move the boat into an up-tide or up-wind position and kill the engine, swinging the boat sideways to the school. This way, the tide, current, or breeze pushes your boat to the school without scaring them with engine noise. This makes it easy to fish or cast from the boat into the school of breaking fish.

76

Hold Line on Ball of Index Finger
When Casting Spinning Tackle

The first crease in your casting index finger seems a natural place to hold spinning line when casting, but you can get a better, smoother release and longer cast with a different technique. For this, pick up the line from the reel spool and hold it for casting on the ball of the end of your index finger. By holding the line this way, there is less possibility of a late or jerky release and thus the result is a longer and smoother cast.

77

Lip Hook Minnows Upside Down for More Action

Use a light jig to lip hook a minnow, but lip hook it upside down. That way, the minnow will constantly try to right itself and create more constant action in the water. A light jig is necessary so the minnow can partially right itself, but has to constantly struggle. If more weight is necessary to get deep, use a heavy in-line sinker about 12 to 18 inches (30 to 45 cm) above the jig and a lip hooked upside down minnow.

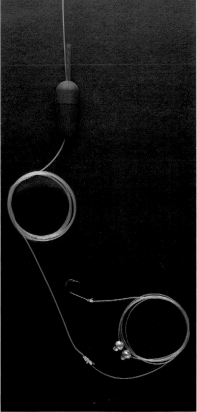

78

Nylon Stocking as Baitfish Holder

Minnows and other baitfish are often hard to hold while trying to put them on a hook. To make this easy, keep a wad of an old nylon stocking handy to grip the minnow. This trick makes it fast and easy to add a minnow to the hook to maximize fishing time and minimize bait rigging time.

79

Use Topo Maps

GPS equipment helps pinpoint your location and allows you to retrace your steps to find your way home or back to camp. If you know how to read them, plain old topographical maps help you find the best fishing locations. Learn about the symbols used on topo maps so you can recognize water, steep hills, shallow valleys, marsh, woodlands, rocks, etc. Once you recognize these, you can tell if a creek in a steep valley might hold trout or be too difficult to traverse or if a marsh surrounds a pond to make it too difficult to reach for fishing. Learn about reading topos and their symbols to learn how you can reach water no one else fishes.

80

Bonus for Paddlers

Trolling in deep, open water may seem like a waste of time, but some anglers who canoe the wilderness lakes of the northern states and Canada know differently. When paddling across open expanses, they toss out a lure, such as a crankbait or minnow plug. Pike, walleyes, lake trout, and smallmouth bass often suspend in open water, feeding on ciscoes, a common baitfish in many of these lakes. Trolling across the middle of a lake is not a high-percentage method, but it produces a surprising number of fish.

80

81

Lure Storage

Got lots of lures? Buy them on special for a backlog inventory? One easy way to store excess lures is to buy some cardboard inventory bins from a stationery store. Bins are available from 12 to 18 inches (30 to 45 cm) deep and from 2 to 12 inches (5 to 30 cm) wide. Mark each bin with the type, brand, or style of lure that it holds for instant refilling of your tackle box. Basic shelving makes it possible to store these bins easily.

82

Try Tailwaters after Heavy Rains

Heavy rains cause most streams to rise quickly and turn muddy. The dirty water usually ruins fishing, but you may be able to salvage your trip by moving to the tailwaters of a good-sized reservoir. Silt settles out in the reservoir, so even after a torrential rain, water flowing from the dam will be relatively clear for some distance downstream. It will stay clear until it is muddied by tributaries.

83

Smooth Fly Casting from a Boat

When fly fishing from a boat, anglers usually drop extra line in loose coils near their feet. On the cast, the line lifts up and zips through the guides—unless you happen to be standing on it. Cutting a cast short this way is especially frustrating when fishing for shallow-water trophies such as tarpon or bonefish.

Your chances are few, so quick, accurate casts are essential. You can eliminate the problem by fishing without shoes so you can feel any line underfoot. Be sure the area is free of hooks and if it's sunny, remember to apply sunblock to protect the tops of your feet from a bad burn.

84

Rubber Band Line Holder

Tie a regular rubber band around your surf rod just above the spinning reel to make a line holder when bait fishing without a bait running drag on your reel. To do this, loop the rubber band around the rod and tie it with a square knot. After making a cast and with the drag adjusted correctly for your line, keep the bail open and slip the line under the rubber band and against the rod by lifting up on the rubber band knotted ends. Keep the spinning reel bail open. When a fish takes the bait, the line pulls out from under the rubber band. This gives you time to get to the rod and throw the bail closed to set the hook.

FISHING WITH KIDS

Fishing can provide a lifetime of enjoyment for your kids, if you get them started right. If you don't, they'll sour on fishing at a young age.

Do whatever seems most fun to the child. Be flexible. Most kids love to bobber-fish. It's fun seeing the bobber go under. If the kid wants to cast big plugs for sunfish, that's okay. It may not be the best way to catch them, but your kid will have fun casting and may just hook a big fish of some other kind.

Don't force your children to go with you if they don't want to. Keep the trip short and don't make them stay when they've run out of patience. You may be able to maintain their interest by bringing along a surprise, such as a toy, book, game, or candy bar. Keep the treat secret and pull it out when they're starting to get bored. But when their interest has clearly waned, head for home. If you make them stay too long, they won't want to go along next time.

Be patient. Make up your mind that this trip is primarily for the kids' enjoyment!

85

Bank on it

Bank fishing gives your kids plenty of room to roam if they lose interest in fishing. For children, a fishing trip can include not only fishing as we know it but also wading, swimming, skipping stones, catching frogs, and chasing butterflies. Allowing kids to engage in these activities helps to ensure a fun fishing trip and an activity they'll want to engage in again.

86

Simplest is Best

Keep the fishing simple for children. Too often we expect kids to enjoy fishing that's way over their heads. No matter how well the fish are biting, you'll have a tough time selling a 7-year-old on fly fishing or backtrolling live-bait rigs. These methods demand too much patience and practice. As your kids grow older and get more interested in the sport, treat them more like adults.

87

Avoid the Middle

The middle of a big lake is the worst place to go, even if the fishing is terrific. Kids soon tire of fishing and don't find much else to keep them interested. Soon they'll want to go home.

88

Watch & Listen

Give your kids plenty of help when it's needed, but don't overdo it. If possible, let them bait their own hook, cast, and reel in the fish. If you do everything, you'll turn them into bored onlookers.

89

Set Hook To Side

To set a hook in a fish properly, set the hook by levering the rod to the side, not overhead. This allows you to use the power of your twisting body to impart force to the hook strike. The lure will more likely stay in the water if the fish misses the lure/hook, keeping the lure near the strike zone to allow the fish to strike the lure again. Just be careful that you do not have a fellow angler to your side who could be hit by the rod or a flying lure.

90

Stay on the Move

Pick an interesting spot to do your fishing, someplace where there are lots of things to see other than water. Try fishing a small lake where you can make periodic trips to shore to break up the day. Or try float-fishing a stream. You're always on the move and there are plenty of sandbars and riffles to explore along the way.

91

Comfort is Important

Be sure children are warm, well-fed, and protected from bugs and sun. They have a much lower tolerance for sun and cold than adults do. Take along extra jackets even though it seems warm outside and remember to bring their sunglasses. Don't force children to go with you in bad weather; you don't want them to associate fishing with being miserable. Be prepared to make frequent bathroom stops.

92

Chum Fish with Scales

One quick and easy way to chum in running water or deep water is to scale a caught fish and chum with the scales. You can chum as you scale the fish or save the scales for chumming later. The scales are bright and attract fish to your boat or fishing location.

93

Hold Fish Properly to Prevent Angler Injury

Spines and teeth can cause angler injuries. It is important to know how to handle fish to prevent jabs and bites that can ruin your angling day. Some fish, such as catfish and white perch, have spines which can cause an infection. To hold catfish, grab the fish with your hand in back of the dorsal fin spine and your fingers around and in front of the two pectoral fin spines. To hold perch, run your hand from the head to the body so the spines lay down to prevent injury. Pike, pickerel and musky and saltwater bluefish, mackerel, and snapper and other toothy fish should be held in back of the gill plate and never near the mouth. With all big fish, use a gaff or net to land them and only hold the head of the fish to stabilize it while removing the hook with pliers or a de-hooker.

94

Safety Rope Saves Rods

Kids get careless and occasionally drop things. If you're constantly worried about losing a rod and reel, you probably won't have much fun and neither will your child. Tie the reel seat to the youngster's wrist or life jacket with a short cord. Then dropping a rod and reel overboard is nothing to get upset about.

Outfit your kid with a comfortable life vest. Kids may not want to wear a bulky Mae West-type life jacket because it is awkward to fish in and not very stylish.

Any Fish Is a Prize for Kids

Fast action is more important than big fish. By kid standards, a dozen sunnies are better than one 5-pound (2.25 kg) bass. Your job is to get them into plenty of hungry, gullible fish. Brag up anything your kid catches. Remember that a fish doesn't have to be a prize by your standards. Any fish is a trophy if you say it is.

Try fishing panfish, especially around spawning time, when the fish are concentrated in shallow water and eager to take live bait or small lures. Or go to a lake stuffed with bullheads. Another good option is white bass fishing, particularly when the bass are chasing baitfish on the surface. They hit hard and you can often catch one on every cast.

Coat Hanger for Bank Fishing

For rod support, carry a wire coat hanger or two when bank fishing. Use them bent to shape to support (stick in the bank) the rod shaft to detect strikes. Stick the untwisted end of the coat hanger into the ground, then bend the top into a "U" or "V" to hold the rod tip section. If possible, make sure the reel does not touch the ground.

Cricket and Grasshopper Bait Bucket

A simple bait container for crickets and grasshoppers can be made by gluing a dowel to the bottom of a coffee can so it sticks up in the center and is about one-half the height of the coffee can. Cover the open top with a square of plastic screening held in place with rubber bands. Cut two crossed slits in the top so you can reach in to grab a cricket while the screening prevents loss of the bait. In most cases, a cricket or grasshopper sits on top of the dowel/stick for you to easily pluck off while reaching through the screening slits. Use plastic screening so you do not scratch your hands as with metal screening.

Make Your Own Dip Net

Buy some tulle at a fabric store to make a simple and quick dip net to gather baitfish. Buy 1 yard (1 m) of this netting-like material. Any width will work, but 36 to 54 inches (1 to 4 m) wide is the best. Make two diagonal crosspieces of lightweight PVC tubing and tie the ends to netting corners. Drill a hole and fasten an eye bolt through the two pieces of PVC where they cross. Tie a light rope to the eyebolt and lower the net into shallow water frequented by minnows. Bait the net with a dough ball or cereal, wait for the minnows, and pull up the net when minnows are eating the bait. To make a more permanent net, fold a strip of cloth over the edges of the netting and sew it in place. Add grommets to the net corners for ropes to hold the net to the frame and finish as above.

Chapter 2

GAMEFISH TIPS

All fish might seem alike, but many species of game fish are markedly different in their habits, habitat requirements, food, and comfort zone or areas.

For example, trout feed actively on small insects, while pike take only large minnows and baitfish. Bass feed on frogs and crayfish, while striped bass feed on almost anything. Trout take actively off of the surface, while carp and catfish feed mostly on the bottom. Many ocean fish cover miles (km) of territory, while freshwater panfish rest comfortably in small ponds. Know the fish and learn from these specific tips for each gamefish type to learn how to fish for them.

LARGEMOUTH & SMALLMOUTH BASS TIPS

99

Wind in Rushes Triggers Bass

When a strong wind begins whipping a bed of bulrushes, largemouth bass move from the cover inside the bed to the windward points, where they ambush prey and smash lures for two to three hours. Then the bass quit feeding and return to heavy cover or move deep.

100

Plastic Surgery Improves Worms

If bass ignore a normal plastic worm, try a high-buoyancy worm made with air bubbles in the plastic, such as a Sportsman's Super Floater, and enhance its action with a razor blade or X-ACTO knife.

Slice the worm lengthwise from the midpoint to the tail. Then slice each half lengthwise again to form four tentacles. Thread the worm on a jig. With the jig head on the bottom, the tentacles wiggle enticingly.

101

Self-Stick Lead Weights

SuspenStrips and SuspenDots are self-stick lead weight strips that can be added to a lure for added weight and faster sinking. They are best used on the belly of a crankbait to make a suspending lure. They can also be used on metal spoons, spinnerbait blades, flat jig heads, and blade baits.

1. Tie a piece of 30-pound (13.5 kg) stiff mono behind the eye of a 1/0 straight-shank worm hook. Run the line through the eye.

102

Mono Loop Fends off Weeds

Texas-rigged worms are weedless, but with the hook buried in the worm, you'll miss fish. A worm hooked on a plain jig head has an exposed hook, so you'll hook more fish but snag more weeds. You want to rig a worm so it's nearly weedless but still allows a good hook set.

2. Slide the worm on the hook and poke the mono into the worm at the hook bend so the mono forms a loop over the hook point. The loop is stiff enough to fend off weeds and brush but supple enough to give on a strike. Fish the worm with a bullet sinker. Set the hook as soon as a bass hits.

103

Spincast Tackle for Skipping Lures Under Docks

If fishing a lot of docks in your bass angling, add a good-quality spincasting outfit to your tackle arsenal. Spincast does not tangle or backlash line and makes it easy to forcefully throw a lure at a low angle under a dock. Often such lures can be cast so they skip on the water surface to the back of the dock area to get bass that otherwise never see a lure.

104

Floating Line Helps Walk the Dog

"Walking the dog"—working a stickbait so it dodges side to side across a surface—is a proven technique for bass. Give the bait a sharp twitch and give it a bit of slack as it veers to one side. When the bait stops, twitch it again and give it slack as it glides in the other direction. Continue the retrieve so the plug dodges side to side (dotted line) as you bring it toward the boat. It's a great way to raise bass out of submerged weeds, brush, or timber.

But you'll run into a problem if you let the bait lie motionless for several seconds. The monofilament sinks and the bait nose-dives rather than darts to the side.

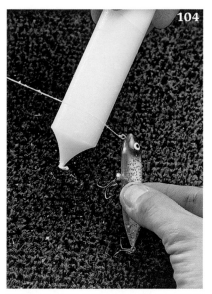

105

Use Black Surface Lure at Night for Bass

A black or black-silhouetted lure shows up best when looking up against a night sky. For this reason, use black lures when fishing at night, particularly when fishing surface lures. Black lures on the surface more closely resemble the silhouette of a struggling minnow, swimming frog, or other meal.

106

Tune Buzzbaits in Moving Car

For maximum action, you can tune your buzzbaits to smooth and spin the blade. You can do this indoors in front of a fan or on the way fishing by holding the buzzbaits, one at a time, out of the car window. (Passengers only, please!)

107

Slap Lure to Remove Weeds

To remove weeds quickly from lures when fishing, slap the lure in a circular glancing stroke against the surface of the water. Do not slap the lure down on the water, but slap it a glancing blow against the surface so the weeds are pulled off. This works with all lures. However, be careful with thin-wall crankbaits and top water lures, since they can be damaged or broken.

Rub a candle (top) or fly floatant over the first 6 feet (1.8 m) of line up from the lure. Either substance floats the line.

108

Better "Pegging" Technique

Plastic-worm anglers peg bullet sinkers with toothpicks to keep the worm and sinker from separating on the cast and retrieve. But the toothpicks jam in the holes, making the sinkers difficult to remove and later reuse without first punching out the toothpick.

109

Worm Scrap for Weedguard

One way to make a weedless spoon like a Johnson Silver Minnow or Weed Wing even better in heavy slop is to use a short length of discarded plastic worm for an added weedguard. While the Johnson Weedless Minnow does have a single weedguard, sometimes slop can get caught between the hook point and end of the weedguard to make the lure not only weedless but also fishless.

110

Fish Shorelines with Dark Bottoms in Early Spring

Shorelines with a dark or muddy bottom warm up fastest in the spring and produce the earliest fishing for bass, panfish, and other lake species. The dark bottom absorbs the heat from the early spring sun to warm the area and the water, attracting fish.

111

Keep Pork Rind Fresh

Left in the open air and hot sun, pork rind quickly dries and loses its suppleness and action. When you set down a pork rind lure for a while but don't want to return the pork to the jar, wrap the pork in a damp rag. When you unwrap the pork later in the day, it will still be soft and full of action.

Slip a rubber sinker stop onto your line before adding the bullet sinker, hook, and worm. To re-rig, simply slide the stop up the line a few inches (cm), snip off the hook, change sinkers, tie on a new hook, and slide the stop back into place.

1. Use a 2-inch (5 cm) length of a thin discarded worm, slide it up onto the weedguard, and then back down over the point of the hook to fill in this guard/hook point gap. To make sure the fish does not miss the hook, run the worm close to the surface of the hook point so the worm tears off when a fish hits.

2. To add more action to the lure, use this technique, but with the curved tail worm so the curved tail extends in back of the lure and acts as a fish-attracting trailer.

112

Keep Curly-Tails from Twisting

If you're bothered by severe line twist after casting with a curly-tail plastic worm, you're not alone. Even if the worm is hooked straight, without a kink in the body, it may twist on the retrieve.

113

Pack Pork in Plastic Bags

Jars of pork rind are bulky. To carry pork in a vest or small tackle box, pack a few pieces and some of the brine in a small resealable plastic bag.

114

Write Off Weeds

Spinnerbaits are a favorite for bass in heavy cover. They're nearly weedless, but the swivel often catches bits of fine weed, stopping the blade. Use a ballpoint pen to keep the swivel weed-free.

115

Secret Humps

River fishermen know that smallmouth bass and walleyes hold behind bridge pilings to get out of the current, so most of these spots are heavily fished. But there's another kind of cover associated with bridges that is harder to spot and is fished less often. As bridge builders sank bridge footings, they would excavate boulders and rubble from the riverbed and dump the material in a pile nearby. Use your depth finder to sound the river bed in the vicinity of the bridge to find these submerged rock piles. Most anglers overlook such spots, yet they make ideal cover for smallmouth, walleyes, and other gamefish.

116

Bang Jigs for Bass

If you're over a school of bass on a rock pile, but ordinary jigging fails to trigger them to strike, get their attention by "banging" a jig.

Drop a heavy jig to the bottom, raise it up a few inches (cm), and let it fall. Continue to bounce it on the rocks with short vertical movements of the rod. It's hard for bass to ignore the repeated clunking.

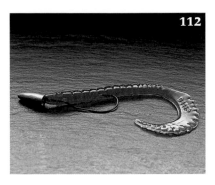

Hook the worm so the curly-tail rides down when the hook point rides up. Make sure the body isn't kinked. If the tails turned up, the worm is much more likely to spin as it moves through the water.

Cut off the last ¾ to 1 inch (1.9 to 2.5 cm) of the pointed top of a ballpoint pen top. Poke or drill a small hole through the tip. Using a needlenose pliers, open up the loop at the end of the spinner arm and remove the swivel and spinner blade. Slide the plastic cone onto the spinner arm. Then reattach the blade and push the cone back along the arm so it covers the swivel (bottom).

117

Add Spice to Spinnerbaits

Many anglers fish shiners for bass, but when the bait dies, they simply throw it away. Instead, you can use the shiner to tip a skirtless spinnerbait. It makes the lure more attractive and also slows the sink rate so you can work near the surface without speeding up the retrieve.

118

Weedguards for Heavy Cover

In slop, thick lily pads, bulrushes, or timber, ordinary weedless jigs still hang up because the nylon bristles don't shield the hook point from the sides. A quick adjustment makes the weedguards work better.

Flare the bristles across the point and heat them with a lighter or match. Be careful not to melt them. When cool, the nylon will stay in the new position.

119

Good Vibrations

Fishing gets tough with a sudden change in weather—the dreaded cold front. Still, cold-front bass aren't impossible to catch. Bass are sure to notice big baits that make strong vibrations in the water. Here are a couple of examples.

A big, single-bladed spinnerbait with a size 6 or 8 Colorado blade produces a strong, slow vibration that can tempt lethargic bass. Put a jumbo pork frog on the hook to slow the sink rate. Cast the lure into heavy cover and retrieve slowly.

Crankbaits run deep enough to reach bass that have been pushed into deeper water by a cold front and the strong vibrations can trigger strikes, even from inactive bass. Cast out a big, sinking, deep-diving crankbait. Reel fast to get it deep, then slow down so it swims along the bottom.

Slip a worm hook with an offset shank onto the spinnerbait hook as a trailer (top). Hook the shiner through the lips with the spinnerbait hook and bind it to the trailer with a rubber band (bottom). The offset shank lets the hook lie flat against the minnow.

120

Stiff Rod Rips Weeds

A rod with good backbone works best for ripping a crankbait through weeds. You can't get enough snap with a soft rod to tear the weeds, so they stay on the lure. But with a stiff rod, you can rip the lure free with one sharp tug.

121

Stick to Bread-and-Butter Spots

After cold fronts, fish the spots that normally produce bass; exploring new water is a bad bet when fish aren't feeding. Usually bass will be in the areas you found them before the front passed. But they may hold tighter to cover or in slightly deeper water.

122

Vertical Jigging from a Distance

Jigging directly below the boat catches bass in cold weather or at other times when fish are inactive. It's hard for a bass to resist the temptation of a jig repeatedly bouncing right in front of its nose. But if the water is clear, you can't park your boat directly over fish without spooking them.

123

Target Shallow Weeds

With a change in weather, many bass head to the thickest weeds available. Some of this cover may be deep, some as shallow as 3 or 4 feet (0.9 or 1.2 m). Make best use of your time by trying the shallow weeds first.

In the shallows you can easily see where the cover is thickest and provides the most security, so you can flip or pitch a jig-and-pig or plastic worm practically on a fish's nose. Getting close in deeper water is far more difficult, because you can't see the nooks and crannies of the cover and aren't so sure where fish are likely to be holding.

124

Use Heavy Sinker in Heavy Weeds for Bass Fishing

When fishing in heavy weeds, it often seems impossible to get a worm through the matted grasses to the fish below. To do this, use a heavy egg sinker or worm weight on the end of the line and immediately above the worm. Sinkers weighing about 1 ounce (28 g), or even larger, are good. Peg the weight to the line so the sinker does not slide along the line if the worm gets hung up in the grass. By pegging the sinker and dropping the sinker several times in a flipping technique to get the sinker through the grass, the worm follows and you often get a hit.

Vertical-jig a ¹⁄₁₆-ounce (1.7 g) squid-tail jig below a large slip bobber, setting the bobber stop to put the jig at the same level as the fish. The large bobber has enough flotation and water resistance that a sharp pull lifts the jig rather than sinking the bobber or pulling it back toward you.

125

Easy-to-Open Pork Rind

As you use pork rind, the brine corrodes the cover of the jar and forms a salty deposit on the threads. As a result, the jar can be impossible to open by hand. Try this trick to keep the cover from sticking.

Spread a thin coat of petroleum jelly on the threads of the cover and jar when you first use the pork rind; repeat occasionally during the season. The petroleum jelly prevents corrosion and lubricates the cover, so it comes off easily.

126

Save Light Tippets

Fly fishermen who stalk small, clear streams for smallmouth bass often find that light tippets used with tiny jigs and poppers are a winning combination. But the continual shock of false-casting even these small lures eventually weakens a clinch knot tied with a 4-pound-test (1.8 kg) tippet. If you don't retie often, you may lose a big fish.

Solve the problem by using a Duncan loop instead of a clinch knot or other knot that snubs down on the hook. The Duncan loop better withstands the shock of false casting a weighted fly. As a bonus, the loop allows small poppers and jigs freer play for better action.

127

Looking for Active Fish

Under cold-front conditions, most anglers slow down their presentation to entice fish that aren't interested in feeding. Some fishermen, however, do just the opposite: they work fast, hoping to find and catch the few fish that are relatively active.

Fish water you know well and move quickly from one proven spot to another, fishing each no more than 10 minutes. Pepper the areas with lures you can work fast, such as spinnerbaits and crankbaits. By covering a lot of water, you should be able to find a few active, catchable bass.

Thread the tippet through the hook eye and then form a loop next to the standing line. Make five turns around one side of the loop and the standing line. Wet the knot and tighten it by pulling on the fly and the free end. Slide the knot to within ¼ inch (6 mm) of the hook eye. Trim.

Clip several bristles at the base with a scissors or nail clipper. A dozen or so fibers remaining protect the hook in thin cover and yet are supple enough to hook most of the fish that hit.

128

Weedguards for Light Cover

In sparse weeds or brush, nylon-bristle weedguards may protect the hook more than is necessary, causing missed strikes.

129

Prevent Line Twist with Bass Bugs

Large bass bugs, especially frog imitations with big splayed legs, may spin in the air as you cast, twisting your leader and line. Attaching the lure to a snap-swivel eliminates line twist but also causes a bug to ride low in the water or sink, ruining the action. Keep twist out of your line without sinking the bug.

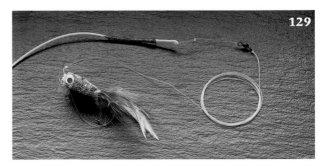

Attach a short piece of 30-pound (13.5 kg) mono to the fly line. Tie the mono to a small swivel; attach the leader to the other end of the swivel. The swivel may sink the tip of the fly line, but it won't affect the bug.

130

"Doodlin'" Brass and Glass

Doodlin'—twitching a Texas-rigged plastic worm along the bottom—catches bass in a lot of situations, but it can be one of the best approaches to try after a cold front has passed. Doodlin' can be even more effective if you add a brass bullet weight and a glass bead to the worm. As you're trolling, drifting, or retrieving, twitch the rod tip rapidly, keeping the worm on the bottom. The brass and glass will click together, making far more noise than an ordinary lead sinker.

Slide a brass bullet weight and a good-sized glass bead onto 6-pound-test (2.7 kg) monofilament. Tie on a worm hook and rig a plastic worm Texas style. Brass is not as dense as lead, so you'll need a larger-than-normal sinker to get down.

131

Finding Weedline Bass

As a cold front passes, bass holding at various depths along a weedline move to the base of the weeds. Inside turns in the weedline are usually best.

132

Double Bait for Big Fish

If you're catching only little walleyes and saugers, you may be using minnows that are too small. Bigger fish often want bigger bait. If you run out of big minnows, there is a way to save the day.

Hook two small minnows on a jig or split-shot rig. Don't bury the hook too deeply or the minnows will jam up in the bend of the hook and won't trail naturally.

133

Dead-Head Worm for Stubborn Bass

After a cold front or at other times when bass are "off the bite," they'll refuse everything you throw at them. Experts advise using a very slow presentation, but when the cold front is severe, this strategy may not work either.

Here's a rig that requires a great deal of patience to fish properly but produces bass when other offerings won't. For best results, keep boat movement to a minimum. Anchor in an area where you were catching bass before the front.

134

Slow and Subtle

Although big, noisy lures can catch cold-front bass, a slow presentation with a small lure also works. Here's one proven method for cold-front bass: rig up with clear, light mono and a 1/16- to 1/8-ounce (1.7 to 3.5 g) tube jig. If the water is deep or cloudy enough that you can put the boat over fish without spooking them, try vertical jigging, which lets you work a lure right in front of fish until one decides to strike.

If the water is clear or shallow and scaring fish is a possibility, cast and jig instead. Either way, work the jig as slowly as you can.

135

Jigging a Worm in Place

Working a Texas-rigged plastic worm slowly through heavy cover is an effective cold-front technique. But even the slowest retrieve may be too fast when bass are off the bite. Here's a way to entice them.

When the worm hangs up on submerged branches or weeds, resist your first reaction to rip it free. Instead, after you feel the sinker hit the obstruction, drop the rod tip a bit so the worm sinks a few inches. Then pull the line tight again to raise the worm. If a bass is around, the action of a worm jigged repeatedly in front of its nose may be too much to resist.

Push a 3- or 4-penny finishing nail into the head of a 4½- to 6-inch (11 to 15 cm) floating worm, then insert a 4/0 worm hook through the middle of the worm. Hold the worm upright after casting by keeping slight tension on the line. Wait up to five minutes before moving the worm. Often, a bass picks it up and hooks itself.

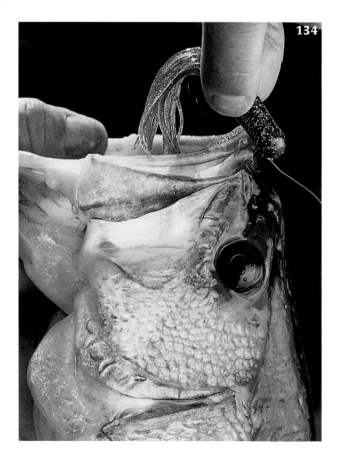

WALLEYE & SAUGER TIPS

136

Jigs for Weed Walleyes

Stocked walleyes spend a lot of time in the thick vegetation usually associated with largemouth bass. You can catch these walleyes by casting jigs into this heavy cover. But ordinary walleye jigs don't work well; the exposed hook point and attachment eye on top of the jig head snag weeds. And most weedless bass jigs are too big.

Try a ⅛-ounce (3.9 g) weedless jig with the attachment eye at the front of the head, which lets the lure slip through weeds easily. Some of these jigs also have a flattened head to slow the sink rate, so you can swim them over very dense weeds.

137

Durable Natural Jig Dressing

If you run out of bait and walleyes refuse artificials, try tipping a jig with throat tissue cut from a walleye you've already caught and kept frozen. The thin flesh wiggles enticingly on the hook, emits natural scent, and is remarkably durable.

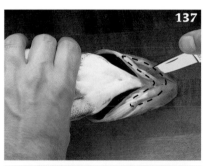

138

Improved Willow Rig

Veteran walleye and sauger anglers often use a willow twig to detect subtle bites while ice fishing. They anchor a 2- to 3-foot (60 to 90 cm) twig in the slush removed from the hole, then center the tip over the hole, about a foot above the water. Then they make a loop in the line and hang it over the tip of the twig. A light bite pulls the willow down slightly; a hard bite bends the willow far enough down so the loop slips off. Normally, line is spread on the ice so the fish can run with no resistance.

139

Don't Drill at Dusk

Many ice fishermen make the mistake of showing up at dusk, just when the walleyes are moving in to feed. When they drill their holes, they spook the fish. You can avoid the problem by drilling your holes an hour earlier.

Cut out the throat tissue by slicing along the dotted lines as shown. Then cut the tissue loose at the point of the chin. Drive the jig hook through the front of the piece of throat tissue (below). The meat there is thicker and tough, so the hook won't tear out.

140

Pinch-on Sinker for Deep Fishing

A simple way to add weight to a weedless spoon to fish deep weeds is to add a pinch-on or slide-on runner center sinker to the single-wire weedguard. This extra weight sinks the spoon rapidly and usually does little or nothing to affect the wobbling action. This only works on single weedguard spoons. Adding weight to one of the guards on a two-wire guard spoons makes the lure unbalanced.

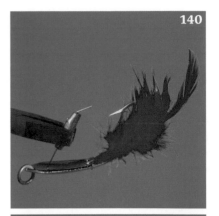

141

Check the Downwind Side

On a windy day, walleye anglers normally fish the windward side of an underwater hump or point. But there are also times when fish feed on the downwind side. On a shallow hump or point, strong wind whips up a great deal of turbulence, causing various kinds of invertebrates to drift off the downwind side of the rocks. Baitfish gather to feed on the small organisms. Then gamefish, including walleyes, largemouth bass, and muskies, move in to feed on the baitfish.

142

A Long Reach Means Fewer Snags

Submerged boulder piles and rocky reefs are top spots for walleyes. But it's nearly impossible to fish a jig or slip-sinker rig in the rocks without getting hung up. You can minimize snags by keeping your line straight up and down, but even then, you'll hang up once in a while. Here's how to improve your chances of freeing a lure if you do get snagged. Use a longer rod so you can reach out farther to change your angle of pull, making it possible to dislodge the hook without repositioning the boat. Some anglers use specially designed spinning rods up to 8 feet (2.4 m) long or they rig a fly rod with a spinning reel.

143

Use Hitchhiker to Add Soft Plastic Trailers To Lures

Hitchhikers are small corkscrew wire shapes with an eye formed on one end. The corkscrew part makes it easy to twist them into the head of a soft plastic. The eye makes it easy to fit onto the hook or screw eye hook hanger of a lure. These work great for soft plastic minnow and shrimp imitations when saltwater fishing and adding a trailer to a bait hook or bucktail.

144

Slow Down Slip-Bobbers

Slip-bobbers are tough to beat when fishing live bait for walleyes. A breeze can make the rig even more effective by slowly moving the bobber and bait through water that might hold fish. Yet a strong wind moves the bobber and bait too fast to interest any but the most active fish. You can slow down the drift and catch walleyes that aren't willing to chase fast-moving bait:

145

Springtime Walleye Magnet

Walleye fishermen know that the fish feed in the shallows in spring because the water there is warmer than in the main body of the lake. The difference may be only a degree or two, but it's enough to attract baitfish and the walleyes soon follow.

But some areas along shore are warmer than others, so they draw more walleyes. Water in a sheltered bay, for instance, warms faster than water along a straight shoreline because the wind can't mix it with deeper, cooler water.

146

Chart Depth While Ice Fishing

Often walleyes school on a small point or in a tiny indentation along the breakline. It takes a lot of depth readings to find these spots and eventhen you may not get a clear picture of the bottom unless you keep track of the depth at each location.

After you sound through the ice or through an ice hole, use the handle of your ice scoop to scratch the depth in the ice or snow. You can even stomp contour lines in the snow, joining holes of equal depths.

Once you have marked the depths and contours, you have a much better understanding of the structure and where fish might be.

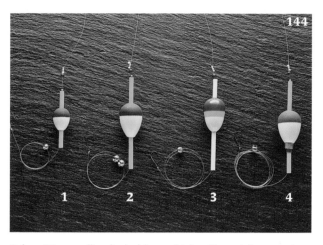

Select (1) a smaller slip-bobber, which will catch less wind and move the bait more slowly than a large float. (2) Use enough weight on your line that the bobber barely floats; this way it is little affected by wind. (3) Choose a wooden float; it's denser than foam so it rides lower, drifts slower, and casts better. (4) Use a bobber weighted with a lead sleeve. It will ride low and drift slowly and the extra weight will increase casting distance.

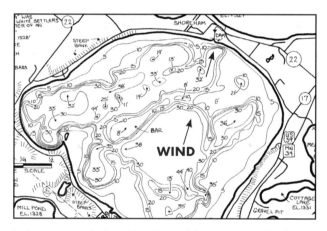

Indentations in the breakline (arrow) function much like bays, but are not obvious from looking at the shoreline. Sunlight heats the surface layer of the lake and if the wind pushes the warm water toward shore, it collects in the depression. An indentation on the downwind side of the lake may have water 10 degrees warmer than nearby shallows.

147

There's More Than One Way to Hook a Leech

Most fishermen hook their leeches in or around the sucker, the large disc on the wide end (tail). This method of hooking works well for most types of fishing, but there are times when other ways are more effective.

148

A Rocky Start for Walleyes

Look for early-season walleyes on rock piles in water less than 10 feet (3 m) deep. The rocks absorb sunlight and warm the surrounding water. Most of the lake is still cold, so walleyes are attracted to these zones of warmer water. These areas appeal to walleyes for another reason: the warmth activates invertebrates, which attract baitfish on which the walleyes feed. Walleyes frequent big boulders later in the year as well. The large rocks cast shadows where the walleyes can hide and avoid bright sunlight.

149

Slip in on Walleyes

The sound of an outboard, the whir of an electric trolling motor, or the clunk of an anchor can spook walleyes off a shallow reef. To approach such a spot silently, anchor at least 50 feet (15 m) upwind and pay out rope until you're within casting range. If you need to check the reef with your depth finder, let your boat blow right over the spot, take your readings, and then move slightly upwind by taking in anchor rope.

150

Cut through Stringy Weeds

Walleyes are sometimes found in stringy weeds, such as coontail. The weeds catch on your line, slide down, and foul your lure. Sometimes you can shake them off during the retrieve, but more often you have to reel in the lure and remove the weeds by hand. Here's an easier way.

Add a short leader of thin multi-strand wire, such as 12-pound-test (5.4 kg) Sevenstrand, between your line and lure. When you feel resistance from a weed, jerk the rod. The thin wire cuts through the stem and the weed falls off the line. The wire leader also ensures that sharp-toothed fish such as northern pike won't bite off your lure.

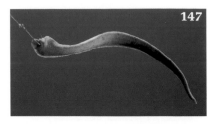

1. Through the sucker. Hooking in or near the sucker is recommended for most casting and trolling. Because you pull the leech backwards, it always tries to swim away.

2. Through the middle. This method is ideal for bobber fishing. The leech is balanced on the hook, so it undulates more than it would if hooked in the end.

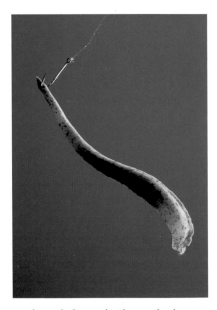

3. Through the neck. This method is best when nipping panfish are a problem. The flesh in the neck region is very tough, making it harder for them to steal your bait.

151

Snag-Resistant Walleye Jig

Walleyes often hang out in snaggy cover where an ordinary jig would hang up almost immediately. You could use a jig with a weedguard to protect the hook, but many of these jigs are often fishless as well as snagless. You can use a jig that will allow you to work a lure over a snaggy bottom, yet there's no weedguard to reduce your hooking percentage.

152

Cure for Balled-Up Leeches

When the water is cold (below 50°F [10°C]), leeches tend to ball up on the hook. Even in warm water, a leech occasionally decides to roll itself up tight. Regardless of what you do, you can't get them to unwind and swim. The problem occurs most often when the leech is hooked through the neck, though some leeches ball up no matter where you hook them. Unfortunately, a balled-up leech is worthless for walleyes.

  Prevent the problem by sliding a short piece of surgical tubing over the collar of the jig. Hook the leech far enough ahead of the sucker so the sucker can attach to the tubing. A leech with its sucker attached to something is not as likely to ball up.

153

Early-Bird Walleyes

Walleyes in heavily used lakes often feed earlier in the day than those in less popular lakes. Speedboaters, jet-skiers, water-skiers, and other commotion drive them into deep water or heavy cover. Often, the traffic stays heavy until dark, and walleyes don't feed much before the lake settles down.

  To catch these early feeders, start fishing at the crack of dawn. The bite may end by breakfast time.

154

Clean Jig Eyes

Most jigs you buy are painted by dipping the entire head. Usually the attachment eye is clogged with paint, so you have to poke a hole to attach your line. But if you use another hook to open the eye, as many anglers do, some paint will remain on the eye. When you tie on your jig, the knot won't snug up properly and the rough edge can fray your line.

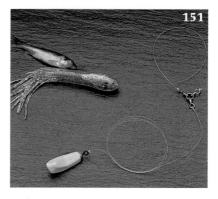

Make a snag-resistant jig by pushing a 3- to 4-inch (7.6 to 10 cm) soft plastic tube body over a floating jig head. Tie the jig head to a three-way swivel with an 8-inch length of monofilament. Attach a 1- to 2-foot (30 to 60 cm) dropper, slightly lighter than your main line, to the swivel; add a walking sinker. Tie the swivel to your main line and tip the jig with a small minnow. Now the jig rides well above bottom and the walking sinker slides over most snags. If you hang up, you lose only the sinker.

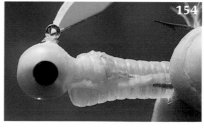

Push the point of a knife blade into the eye and give it a half-twist. Usually, all of the paint chips away from the eye. If not, scrape away any that is left to make a smooth surface for your knot.

155

Reuse Soft Plastics

Don't discard old chewed-up soft plastics while fishing. Use them to make new lures by welding parts together. Separate the parts you can use, particularly heads and tail portions that are undamaged. For best results, use an alcohol lamp or flame that you can set on a work bench rather than having to hold while welding lure parts. Check the parts of the two lures you want to weld and if necessary trim them for a proper fit.

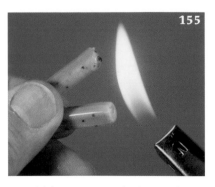

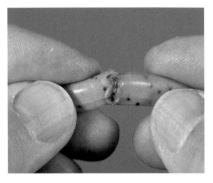

1. Hold the two cut ends close to the flame until they develop a liquid-like molten surface.

156

Free-Standing Stinger

Walleyes often nip at a jig and minnow without getting hooked. Many anglers tie a small treble to the bend of the jig hook and imbed this "stinger" in the minnow's tail. But even light mono between the jig and treble inhibits the action of the bait. And the line often wraps around the minnow, cinching it into a half-circle and ruining its action. Here's a better way.

Tie a size 14 or 16 treble hook to the bend of the jig hook with a short length of stiff line, such as Mason hard mono, 15-pound-test (6.75 kg) or heavier. The stiff line holds the treble straight out behind the jig, so you don't need to hook it in the minnow. The bait moves freely, as if the stinger weren't there at all. Yet when a fish nips the tail, it gets hooked.

2. Immediately remove them from the flame and stick them together for an instant weld. Do not touch the molten plastic; you can also wear utility gloves to prevent burns.

157

Go Light after a Cold Front

Walleyes and saugers don't feed much following a cold front. But they may nip at a small, slow-moving bait. Here's a trick that can put a few walleyes in your boat when fishing really gets tough.

Spool a light spinning outfit with 2- to 4-pound (0.9 to 1.8 kg) mono, tie on a 1/16- or 1/32-ounce (1.7 or 0.9 g) jig, and tip it with a small minnow or leech. Use a trolling motor to keep your boat over a spot where you suspect fish are holding, then drop the jig to bottom. Lift and lower it slowly, move it in very short hops, or just hold it steady; set the hook if you feel a tap or the line tightens. One problem: light jigs are tough to fish in windy weather.

NORTHERN PIKE & MUSKIE TIPS

158

Add Flash to Muskie Lures

Muskies are notorious for following lures to the boat and turning away at the last minute without striking. If you are getting follows but no strikes, try dressing up the lure with a small spinner. The added flash and vibration is often all it takes to trigger a strike.

159

Go Deep for Big Summertime Pike

Fishermen catch plenty of good-size pike in shallow weedy bays in spring, but when the water warms up, they get nothing but "hammer handles" in these areas. The lack of big pike in summer has led to the mistaken belief that big pike lose their teeth or have sore mouths in summer and don't feed. But in reality, they're feeding more than ever.

The main reason for the scarcity of big pike in summer is that anglers aren't fishing deep enough. As pike get larger, they prefer cooler water. In some cases, they'll stay in shallow water and congregate around spring holes, artesian wells, the mouths of trout streams, or other sources of cold water. But if there are no point sources, pike have no choice but to go deep.

If there is adequate oxygen in the lake depths, they'll go as deep as 50 feet (15 m) and occasionally down to 100 (30 m). Lake trout anglers sometimes catch big pike. At these depths, they're generally feeding on good-sized baitfish, such as ciscoes and whitefish, and you'll have to use similar-sized baits to catch them.

160

Skimmer for Ice Fishing

A regular skimmer, such as is used for cooking, is an ideal accessory for ice fishing. Use the skimmer to remove chunks of ice from each ice hole. Plastic ones are best. You can slightly flex them to crack off any build-up of ice that might develop as you use it.

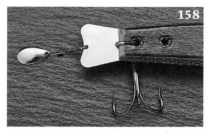

1. Jerkbaits with metal tail blades, such as Suicks, can be modified by drilling a small hole at the center of the rear edge of the tail blade. Add a split ring, a snap-swivel and a size 0, 1, or 2 spinner. The greater drag of sizes larger than this inhibits the lure's action. The snap allows you to easily remove or change the spinner blade.

2. Glidebaits and other jerkbaits without metal tail blades, such as Reef Hawgs and Eddie Baits, can also be fitted with a spinner blade. Remove the rear treble hook. Then replace it with a split ring, a snap-swivel, and a size 0, 1, or 2 spinner blade.

161

Spokes for Spinners

A lot of muskie and pike fishermen make their own spinnerbaits and in-line spinners. Most of the components are readily available from specialty fishing tackle stores and mail-order firms. But you may have trouble finding the stiff, heavy stainless steel wire (at least 0.06 inch [1.5 mm]) if you need to make really large spinners and spinnerbaits. If the wire is too light, fish bend it and the spinners won't spin properly. A ready source of heavy wire: bicycle wheel spokes. The rustproof spokes are available in any bicycle shop.

162

More Hookups on Jerkbaits

Jerkbaits account for plenty of good-sized pike and muskies, especially in fall. But many fishermen work jerkbaits too erratically. They sweep the rod 3 to 4 feet (1 to 1.2 m) at a time, causing the lure to dodge rapidly from side to side. As a result, fish often miss the lure. Here's a better way.

Work the lure with smooth, slow, and regular 2-foot (60 cm) sweeps of the rod tip. The lure will still have enough swimming action to attract pike and muskies, but they'll have an easier time catching it and you'll get more hookups.

Drill a hole near the end of the lip and insert a split ring; attach your leader. The plug will run just under the surface and weeds slip down the line and pass under the plug, rather than hang up on the lip.

163

Weed-Resistant Pike Plugs

Pike are suckers for big, metal-lipped plugs such as Pikie Minnows, but when the fish are lurking in shallow weeds, these plugs are impossible to use. They run too deep and the lip collects weeds.

You want to modify these plugs so they run shallower and don't pick up as many weeds.

164

Muskies after Dark

Boat traffic and fishing pressure can force muskies to feed at night. Successful fishermen change their habits, too. Fish the same areas you would during the day and try shallower areas as well. Use bucktails or jointed plugs, working them with a steady retrieve so the fish can easily home in on them.

165

Weight Bucktails Quickly

Fishermen often weight bucktails to make them run deeper or to cast farther into a stiff wind. But sinkers added to the line makes casting awkward; the sinker and lure twirl like a bolo. You can eliminate tangles by adding weight directly to the lure.

166

Finer Points of Figure-Eighting

Muskies are notorious for following a lure to the boat. Good muskie anglers know how to figure-eight a lure to get the fish to strike. But the technique involves more than just sweeping the rod back and forth through the water. Done poorly, figure-eights result in little more than good arm exercise. Done right, they can more than double your muskie catch. Here are some tricks the experts recommend:

- Use a heavy-duty baitcasting reel with the drag set tight. When a muskie follows your lure to the boat, thumb the spool and push in the free-spool button. Then, should a big fish strike next to the boat, you can set the hook and give line when the fish runs.
- When you see a muskie behind your lure, it's important to read its mood to determine how to proceed. If the fish is "hot," you stand a good chance of enticing it to strike. But if it's only mildly interested, you may be better off leaving it alone.
- Watch the fish's head; if it stays within a few inches (cm) of the lure and the mouth is opening and closing, the fish is hot. Begin tracing a big figure eight with the rod tip. The lure should be about 2 feet (60 cm) under water. If the fish continues to follow but doesn't strike, bring the lure back over its snout. This maneuver often triggers a strike.
- If you see a fish following a few feet (m) behind the lure and swimming lazily, chances are it's not ready to strike. You may want to try one or two figure eights, but if the fish doesn't respond, don't continue. You may end up spooking the

Attach a small bell sinker of the appropriate weight to the split ring or wire loop that holds the treble hook. These sinkers make changing or removing weight easy.

fish. Instead, note the precise location. Then come back and try again later. By that time, the fish may be in a more aggressive mood.
- To make a muskie take the lure, do everything you can to keep it away. Many fishermen make the mistake of slowing the lure when they see a fish following, but this is a sure way to make the fish lose interest. Slow down only when the fish quits following, then speed up again. Sometimes the change in speeds will bring the fish back.
- If a muskie follows a surface lure to the boat, don't figure-eight the lure on top. It's nearly always a waste of time. Even if you're using a surface crawler with no underwater action at all, plunge the rod tip into the water and figure-eight the lure a couple feet beneath the surface.

167

Protect Hands from Sharp Teeth

The needle-sharp teeth of pike and muskies and the large hooks you use to catch these fish are a constant danger and can inflict serious wounds in an instant. Protect your hands with heavy buckskin gloves while landing and unhooking these fish. The hooks aren't likely to penetrate the thick leather.

168

Bucktails with Spice

More muskies are caught on bucktails than on any other lure. But there is a way to make bucktails work even better

169

Catch the Biggest Muskies

Casting bucktails and jerkbaits around shallow weedbeds and rock piles accounts for plenty of muskies, but not the biggest ones.

Muskies larger than 30 pounds (13.5 kg) spend most of their time deeper than 25 feet (7.5 m), if there is adequate forage at that depth. They're not likely to leave this zone to chase a lure skimming overhead, so you'll have to get the lure down to their level.

Troll slowly with a large, deep-diving plug, letting out line until you feel the lure hitting bottom regularly. Then reel in a few feet so it hits just once in a while. Point the rod straight back as you troll. When a big fish hits, the line is straight from reel to plug, and the hook set is automatic.

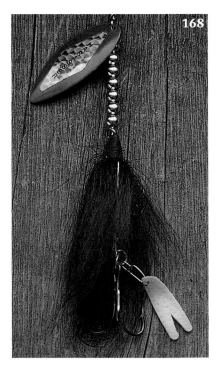

Add a split ring and snap to the wire loop holding the rear treble. Clip a 2-inch (5 cm) white split-tail pork rind onto the snap. If necessary, trim the rind at the leading end and punch a new hole. The rind should stick only ½ inch (13 mm) beyond the bucktail. If you attach the rind directly to the treble and it trails back too far, muskies may strike short.

170

Continuous Figure Eight

This unique two-person procedure has produced dozens of 30-pound-plus (13.6 kg) fish for northern Wisconsin muskie experts. It would work for muskies anywhere.

While one person casts, another figure-eights alongside the boat. When the first person completes his retrieve, he starts figure-eighting and the other person makes a cast. This way, someone is figure-eighting at all times.

The continuous motion evidently arouses the curiosity of big muskies. Even fish that haven't been seen following the retrieving lure suddenly appear and strike the figure-eighted lure.

171

Split Rings Improve Hooking

Muskies and big pike often manage to throw the hook by twisting and thrashing against the weight of a plug. Improve your chances of landing the fish by inserting split rings between the lure and trebles. The rings allow the hooks freer play so big fish can't twist free or bend hooks as easily.

172

Improve Glidebait Action

A wire leader deadens the action of a glidebait, such as an Eddie Bait or Reef Hawg. But you can increase the glide and the side-to-side motion by inserting a split ring (arrow) between the leader and the bait. The ring allows freer play between the steel leader loop and the eye of the plug.

If you're using heavy line and are concerned about the strength of the connection, solder the ring, making sure to file all rough edges that would inhibit movement of the lure. Or you can fit a small split ring inside a larger one.

173

A Stinger for Pike Plugs

When a big pike or muskie grabs a large wooden plug, it's difficult to get a good hook set because their teeth penetrate the wood, preventing you from moving the plug enough to sink the hooks. You can rig a 4-inch (10 cm) wire leader with a snap at one end and a treble hook at the other. Clip the snap to the eye at the nose of the lure. Lay the treble along the plug's back and secure the hook with a rubber band. The treble should be big enough to hold a large fish, but not heavy enough to throw the plugs out of balance.

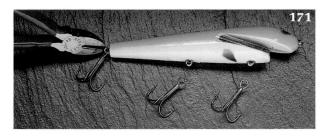

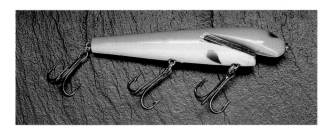

1. Cut off the old treble hooks or remove them by opening the eye of the hook hanger.

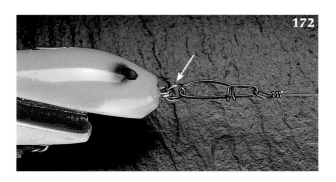

2. Add split rings or double split rings and new trebles; close the eye of the hook hanger.

174

Keeping the Kinks Out

Many anglers use twisted multi-strand steel leaders to keep pike and muskies from biting through the line. But these leaders easily get kinks that are impossible to remove. Then, as you work a lure, the leader flexes at the kind, eventually weakening and perhaps breaking as you play a fish. Get around the problem this way. Buy single-strand leaders or make them yourself from stainless steel wire. It kinks less than twisted wire and kinks that do form are easier to remove. The leader is no heavier, but remains stronger.

175

Prevent Bait Tangles

Monofilament line absorbs water and sinks, sometimes causing problems for bobber fishermen. When you fish a big minnow below a bobber, the bait may swim near the surface, crossing the submerged line between the rod tip and bobber and causing a tangled mess. Even if the sucker doesn't cause a tangle, the sag in the line may prevent a good hook set. You can solve the problem by applying candle wax or fly floatant to the line. The mono floats and stays out of the way of the swimming baitfish.

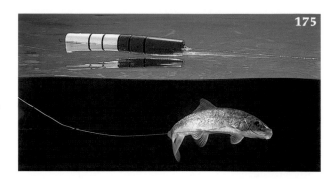

176

Jerking Live Bait for Pike

This unusual but effective method for big pike and muskies combines the action of a jerkbait with the appeal of live bait.

Hook a 6- to 10-inch (15 to 25 cm) sucker minnow upward through only the snout with a 2/0 to 5/0 short-shanked bait hook attached to a foot-long (30 cm.5) wire leader. Cast the minnow with a heavy baitcasting or spinning outfit.

Retrieve the sucker with 2-foot (60 cm) jerks, occasionally pausing to let the bait glide and roll. When you see or feel a strike, wait until you think the fish has swallowed the bait before setting the hook.

Where it is legal, you can rig a small treble hook as a stinger, joining it to the eye of the other hook with a 6-inch (15 cm) section of wire. Hook one prong of the treble in the tail. With this rig, set the hook immediately.

When it is necessary to sink the bait several feet, pinch a large split-shot to the wire leader, several inches (cm) above the nose of the sucker.

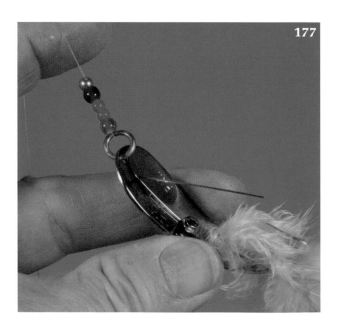

177

Add Beads to Line

One way to add color and a little noise to the front of a weedless spoon is to buy colored beads from your tackle shop or local craft store and slide a few on the line before tying the line to the spoon. The beads add color, protect the knot from damage, and also help to keep weeds and algae off of the line and spoon. Red beads are most popular for this, but any color bead can be used.

178

Better Hook Sets with Big Bait

Anglers sometimes use suckers more than a foot long (30 cm) to catch trophy pike and muskies. These baitfish are usually hooked through the nose, but the thick snout of a really large sucker fills up the hook gap and makes a good hook set difficult. Here are two ways to rig these big baitfish so the hook point remains exposed and the bait stays alive. With either of these methods, you'll have to pause long enough for the fish to swallow the bait before attempting to set the hook.

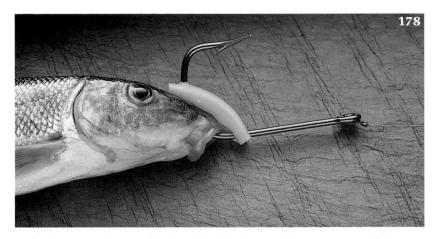

Method 1: Open the gap of the hook slightly; this way the point is more likely to hook a fish and less likely to get buried in the bait. Thread on a "keeper" made of a strip of surgical tubing or a heavy rubber band to keep the sucker from sliding up and down the hook shank. Hook the sucker upward through the snout only, not both lips, to keep more of the hook point exposed. Finally, slide the other end of the rubber onto the hook.

Method 2: Thread a large needle with a foot of heavy braided Dacron fishing line. (1) Push the needle through the eye sockets of the sucker. Draw the line through the head of the bait and (2) tie the ends together to form a loose loop. Trim the ends. (3) Insert a large hook in the loop and twist it several times so the line tightens across the head of the bait. (4) Slip the hook under the taut line and adjust it so the point rides up.

TROUT & SALMON TIPS

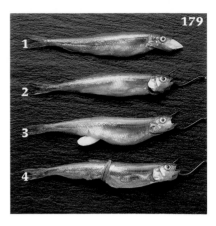

179

Peanuts Give Bait a Lift

Lake trout take dead smelt or ciscoes lying on the bottom, but these baits are more effective when floated up a foot or two (30 to 60 cm). Because lakers are usually found in very deep water, using a slip bobber to suspend the bait is not practical.

Here's a way to float dead bait just off the bottom, where it's visible and appears to be barely alive. It works not only for lakers, but also for big pike.

Stuff a (1) Styrofoam packing peanut inside the mouth of the bait and (2) run the hook through both lips to keep the mouth shut. If more flotation is needed to make the bait float, (3) cut a small slit in the belly and stuff another peanut or two into the abdomen. If the bait is small, use pieces of a peanut. (4) Slip a rubber band over the fish or tie mono around the bait to keep the peanut in the body. Fish the bait 2 feet (60 cm) behind a ½- to 1-ounce (14 to 28 g) sinker.

180

Wormin' for Salmon

During their life at sea, chinooks, cohos, and other Pacific salmon eat small eels of various kinds. Once the salmon enter rivers to spawn, they no longer feed, but they still strike lures resembling eels. As a result, they can be caught on the curly-tailed worms normally used for bass.

Hook a 3- to 5-inch (7.6 to 13 cm) worm on a stout-hooked jig heavy enough to run just off the bottom. Bright or fluorescent colors are usually best, but black and purple work well on bright days.

Anchor your boat above a holding area, then angle your cast down and across the river. Let the current swing the worm in front of the salmon. Or troll the worm through deep water on bends or by creek mouths. Salmon usually hit these lures hard; set the hook as soon as you feel the strike.

181

An Ant for All Seasons

If rising trout won't take an exact imitation of the insects that are emerging, try this trick.

Tie on a black ant pattern that is smaller than the insects the trout are eating. Cast upstream and fish the ant on a dead drift. Trout that reject exact imitations often take small ant patterns, even during winter and early spring, when no real ants can be found. Using a fly that's smaller than the natural works with other patterns, too.

When matching a hatch with a dry fly, it's usually better to use a size smaller than you think you should. Why? First, we overestimate the size of insects in the air. Second, the hackle of a dry fly makes it look larger than a natural with the same length body and wing.

182

Keep Reels Dry When Wading

Wading anglers who fish with a fly rod or long spinning rod are familiar with the problem: to unwrap line from the rod tip or restring the tip section of the rod, you must dunk the reel in the water to reach the last few guides. But then sand gets in your reel. Immersion also caused the drags of some reels to slip.

You can avoid these problems by pulling the rod apart at the ferrule. Now you can untangle the line from the end of the rod. Sod or string up the tip section without putting the reel in the water.

183

Easy-to-See Strike Indicators

Even fluorescent strike indicators can be tough to see in cloudy or hazy weather when you're squinting into the brightest part of the sky.

184

"Unmatch" the Hatch to Take Trout

Sometimes, even dedicated match-the-hatch fly fishermen have to admit defeat. If trout refuse a fly intended to match the insects on the water, here's a trick that may provoke a strike.

Instead of dead-drifting a dry fly, give it a twitch or two or let the line belly out so the fly skates across the surface. Another option: try a fly that differs from the naturals in size, shape and color.

Trout closely inspect and often reject a fly that is almost, but not quite, identical to the insect that is hatching. But they will hit something that is completely different.

Color one end of a strike indicator with a black waterproof marker to provide a dark silhouette. Now, in any light, at least half of the indicator will be visible.

185

Snagproof Salmon Flies

Standard salmon streamers and wet flies are tied to ride with the wing up and the hook point down. But a fly tied this way hangs up easily and is likely to snag a salmon if the leader drifts over the fish's back during the retrieve. Fighting foul-hooked salmon takes time better spent fishing and if you break off, you lose leaders and flies. Even if you don't foul-hook the fish, it may feel the hook across its back and dart away. Some fly-fishermen have borrowed from saltwater anglers to avoid snagging bottom or the fish.

Tie your favorite streamer patterns upside down, like bonefish flies. The hook rides point up and is protected by the wing.

186

Watching Hard-to-See Flies

It's important to watch the drift of a dry fly so you can detect strikes and set the hook. But there are times glare or darkness makes it hard to see dry flies, especially those that imitate small naturals, such as midges.

187

Dacron Backing Saves Fly Reels

Steelheaders often drift flies or bait along the bottom in swift current using a long fly rod rigged with monofilament. The line is stripped off by hand rather than cast off the reel. Many anglers prefer a fly reel to a spinning reel, because the loose loops that form when lobbing and drifting a bait are less likely to tangle on its smaller handle and more compact form. But don't fill a fly reel only with monofilament. Mono stretches under the tension of loading the line or reeling in a fish. Then it constricts on the spool, exerting force not only against the arbor but the sides of the spool as well. This sideways force may cause the spool to spread and bind against the frame.

To avoid ruining your fly reel, fill it to within ½ inch (13 mm) of the pillars with braided Dacron line, which stretches very little. Top off the spool with about 100 yards (91 m) of 8- to 12-pound (3.6 to 5.4 kg) mono, joining the mono to the Dacron as shown.

188

Outsmart "Educated" Salmon

You're fishing for Atlantic salmon and you get a rise, but the fish ignores the fly on subsequent casts. You change flies several times in an effort to attract the fish, but nothing works. Before you leave that fish, tie on the same fly that drew the rise. Often the salmon strike immediately.

189

Find Trout Lies Quickly

Fly fishermen can improve their success by learning where the trout are before they start fishing. Catch a few terrestrial insects, such as grasshoppers, crickets, or beetles. Toss them into the stream and watch them carefully. When a trout grabs one, note the location so you'll know where to cast your fly.

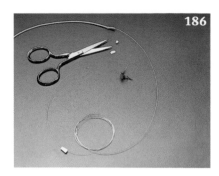

Wrap half of an adhesive foam strike indicator (the kind used by nymph fishermen) around the tippet, about 10 inches (25 cm) above the fly. Trim it to the size of a BB so it doesn't hinder casting or spook fish. This small piece of white foam will be much easier to follow in poor light than a tiny, dark fly. When a fish takes the fly, the foam disappears.

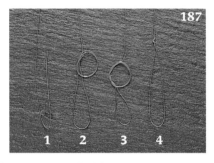

1. First, tie a double surgeon's loop in the end of each line by (1) doubling over the line, (2) tying an overhand knot with the loop, and (3) pushing the loop through the knot a second time. (4) Pull tight and clip the end.

2. Then, interlock the two loops by threading the mono loop through the Dacron loop and then passing the mono spool through the mono loop. Pull the loops tight. Then fill your reel with mono to within ⅛ inch (3 mm) of the pillars.

190

Double-Duty Steelhead Plug

West Coast steelheaders often use a crankbait, such as a Magnum Hot'N Tot, to carry bait to the bottom of a steelhead run and also to act as an attractant. Normally, the hooks are removed so they don't foul the trailing bait rig. But then you miss the occasional steelhead that strikes the plug.

Rig the crankbait so you can catch fish on the plug as well as the bait.

191

Better Fly Floatant

Silicon gel fly pastes are handy, but difficult to apply to flies evenly and thoroughly. If you don't apply enough, the fly won't float long. If you dab on too much, the hackles, wings, and tail mat down. What you need is a dressing that cleans and treats every part of the fly, evaporates quickly, and floats a fly a long time. Make a dressing that does just that.

192

A Shoulder to Lean On

Slippery rocks and swift water can make wading treacherous. If you're fishing a stream with a friend, wade across fast riffles or runs while gripping each other's vest or jacket. Your footing and balance will be much surer than if you had tried to wade alone.

193

Stopping a Strong Run

When hooked, a big salmon or steelhead makes a swift, powerful run, sometimes stripping off a hundred yards (91 m) of line or more. If you're fishing in a boat, you may have no choice but to turn around and chase the fish. When wading in a stream, you may have to follow the fish downstream. If you can't, it will break off in seconds. Here's a trick that stops a streaking fish nine times out of ten.

Give the fish complete slack. They run because they feel resistance; when there is no resistance, they usually stop. In a stream, they often swim back upriver. Once you gain back some line, you can put the pressure on again.

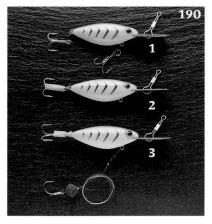

Remove the (1) front treble and split ring; then remove the rear treble, leaving the split ring on the plug. (2) Slide a short piece of surgical tubing over the rear hook shank and then reattach the hook. (3) Slide the tubing forward so it covers the rear eye, split ring, and hook eye and fasten the desired bait rig to the front eye. The tubing causes the treble hook to stick straight off the rear of the plug so it doesn't foul the trailing bait rig.

Mix one part silicon gel fly floatant with three parts lighter fluid. Store the mixture in a small jar or squeeze bottle, after first adding a little to the bottle to make sure the plastic doesn't dissolve. Squeeze a drop or two directly onto the fly or apply it with your fingers or a toothpick. The lighter fluid evaporates in seconds, leaving a thin coat of the gel on the hackles and body of the fly.

194

Add Yarn to an Egg Loop

Fresh spawn with a bit of bright yarn is a top steelhead and salmon bait. Most anglers snell the eggs and yarn on the hook. But a snell may pinch off the eggs. An egg loop won't pinch off spawn, but it doesn't draw tight enough to hold the yarn. Here's how you can add yarn to an egg loop:

195

Get a Grip on Salmon

Anglers wade fishing streams for Atlantic or chinook salmon often have to fight through brush and hike over rough terrain to reach their fishing spots. A large landing net catches in brush and is a pain to carry.

Some fishermen choose to leave the nets at home and "tail" their salmon by leading the fish close, grabbing the base of its tail and quickly lifting. Atlantics and chinooks have stiff outer rays in the tail that keep it from folding and slipping through your fingers. Tailing is often used for fish up to about 20 pounds (9 kg), though the size you can handle depends on practice and the strength of your grip.

196

Stack the Right Spoons

Stacking spoons on downriggers (attaching two or three spoons on the same downrigger cable) is one of the best ways to improve your odds of catching salmon. But anglers who stack spoons of different weights risk tangling their lines unless they know how to arrange their spoons properly.

If you want to stack heavy trolling spoons along with light spoons, always run the heaviest spoons closest to the bottom. If you stack heavy spoons above the light ones, the heavy spoons sink faster when you make a turn or slow down, fouling the lines that go to the light spoons.

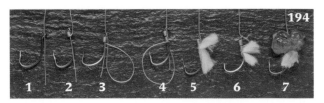

Tie an egg loop by threading (1) the end of a 24-inch (60 cm) piece of mono through a hook with an upturned eye. (2) Wrap the long end around the shank and tag end six to eight times. (3) Make a loop, then push the long end back through the eye. (4) Hold the wrapped portion while making six or eight more wraps over the tag end and the other line. (5) Insert a small bunch of yarn in the rear loop, then pull on the long end of the line to tighten the knot and secure the yarn. Trim the tag end of the line. (6) Grasp the yarn in a single bunch and clip it with a scissors to form an egg-like ball. (7) Cut a marble-sized ball of spawn from a skein of fresh salmon eggs, leaving as much of the membrane as possible to hold the eggs together. Open the front loop of the knot, slip the eggs inside, and pull the loop tight, securing the eggs to the hook. The knot won't pinch off the eggs, yet the rear loop will hold the yarn firmly in place.

Hook the worm on a gold, silver, or fluorescent panfish ice fly. For best casting, use 2- or 4-pound (0.9 to 1.8 kg) mono on an ultralight spinning rig. The ice fly and worm will cast as a unit, improving your accuracy.

197

Ice Jigs Score in Streams

If you're fishing worms for stream trout, you'll generally need a bit of weight to aid casting and get the worm down to the fish. Pinching a split-shot or two several inches above the bait does the trick, but the shot and hook revolve around one another on the cast, making accurate placement difficult. Here's a way to make your bait easier to cast and also more appealing to the fish.

198

Pre-Tied Tippets Save Time

Some predictable mayfly hatches occur late in the evening. The hatch and the fishing can turn on suddenly and proceed at a furious pace. When it's dark and the fish are feeding aggressively, it's easy to break off a fly on a fish or snag it in the brush. Because these hatches may peak and end within minutes, the time-consuming task of trying to tie on a small fly in the dark is especially frustrating and even a small flashlight can ruin what night vision you do have.

A little preparation at home can save time and prevent frustration once you're on the stream.

199

Follow Shifting Plumes

Big-lake salmon and trout anglers know that the fish are strongly attracted to plumes of water flowing into the lake from rivers and even very small creeks. These plumes carry the scent of the streams where the fish hatched or were stocked. The river water also creates a mixing zone in the lake where the water temperature is often ideal.

But many fishermen do not realize that winds can shift the plumes around. One day the plume is blown north, the next day south. The fish follow the plumes as the wind moves them about. So if you fish the same area day after day, you may be on fish one day and nowhere near them the next.

You can locate these shifting plumes by looking for the change in color between lake and river water. But sometimes, the change is hard to see. If the river is large, you may be able to find the plume with the help of a surface-temperature gauge. A small creek, however, has too little flow to have much effect on the lake temperature. In that case, try to anticipate where wind will blow the creek water. Be sure to fish the windy side of downwind points and piers, where the water is most likely to collect.

200

Ski Wax Tames Dubbing

Spinning short animal hair onto a thread, a process called "dubbing," is the first step in forming the bodies of many dry flies, wet flies, and nymphs. However, the process can be tricky and messy, especially for a beginning fly tier, because short hair doesn't adhere very well to the thread. Instead, it sticks to the tier's fingers or falls into his lap. You want to make the hair stick so it's easier to spin onto the thread.

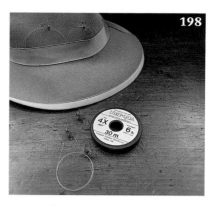

Attach 2-foot (60 cm) tippets to several flies of the pattern you think you'll need. Tie a double surgeon's loop in the other end of each tippet. Coil the tippets and tuck them in your hat band, sandwich them in a Velcro fastener on your vest, or hook the flies in a fleece patch and let the tippets dangle. Tie a double surgeon's loop in the end of your leader, and loop on one of the pre-tied tippets and flies. This way, if you break off a fly, you can simply replace the tippet. Changing tippets is much faster and easier than tying small flies, especially if it's dark and you're surrounded by hungry trout.

1. Apply a light coating of soft (warm-weather) cross-country ski wax to several inches of thread.

2. Dab on the hair. Pinch the thread below the hair; roll the thread between your thumb and forefinger to form yarn.

201

Clean Felts to Prevent Invasive Diseases

Trout fishermen in particular are aware that invasive diseases such as whirling disease and didymo algae are invading our waters and killing fish, particularly trout. To prevent the spread of these diseases, make sure that you empty the bilge in your boat or canoe before leaving a fishing area and that you clean your waders and other gear before leaving an area to try a new river or spot. Felt-soled waders are particularly damaging since they hold the spores of these invasives to infect new areas. To clean waders, make sure that you remove all mud. Allow them to dry for several days before using in a new area. If going to a new area immediately, use a bath of dilute chlorine bleach to kill any of these or other diseases.

202

"Cheater" Increases Odds

When using downriggers, more lures mean more fish. But that requires extra rods. You want to fish two lures on a rod, each at a different depth, by using a "cheater".

203

Cheap No-Slip Soles

The algae-covered boulders in some trout streams are as slick as grease. With ordinary rubber-soled boots you can fall flat on your face. Many anglers buy expensive boots or waders with felt soles to get traction on slippery rocks, but here's a cheap way to improve your footing with waders you already own.

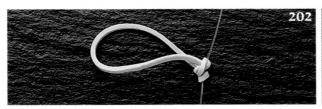

Loop a rubber band (left) to your line after letting it out, attaching it to a release and lowering the cannonball down about 10 feet (3 m). To prevent the rubber band from slipping, wrap it around the line twice, pushing one loop through the other and cinch it tight. Rig a cheater (right) by running one end of an 8-foot (2.4 m) mono leader with a second lure through the rubber band; clip the leader snap to your line. The rubber band keeps the leader from sliding up and down. Lower the downrigger ball to the desired depth. When a fish strikes, the rubber band breaks. The cheater snap slides down the main line, pops the release, and continues sliding until it jams against the lower lure. Now you have a direct pull on the fish.

1. Grind the lugs off the soles of your boots with a coarse-grained belt or disk sander to provide a roughed-up but flat surface for gluing.

2. Trace the outline of the boots onto a scrap of indoor-outdoor carpet. Scrape any foam backing off the carpet with a wire brush.

3. Coat the sole and carpet with a strong adhesive. Follow the directions that come with the glue. Tape on the soles until the adhesive sets.

204

Offbeat Colors for Steelhead

When drift-fishing for steelhead or salmon, many fishermen use bright or fluorescent yarn. Fish probably mistake these flies for spawn. But don't limit yourself to old standards such as orange, pink, and chartreuse. Here are some other colors and color combinations that often work when the usual colors don't.

205

No-Cling Guides for Drift Fishing

When you drift for steelhead or salmon, it pays to use a long rod, because a long rod holds the line off the water better than a short one, making it easier to control line during the drift. But if you use a fly rod and mono, as many anglers do, the snake guides let the line slap against the rod shaft. In rainy weather, the mono clings to the wet rod, cutting the cast short. You can avoid the problem by modifying your existing fly rod or building a new one especially for drift-fishing.

206

Interchangeable Sinking Tips

Many fly-fishermen use sink-tip lines to get streamers or nymphs down to trout feeding near the bottom. The sink rate and length of the sinking portion varies from line to line. The best combination for one situation won't necessarily be the best choice in another. You could solve the problem by carrying several different sink-tip lines. There's a cheaper and more convenient way.

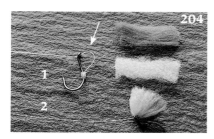

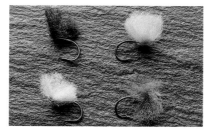

1. Insert (1) two pieces of contrasting yarn into the loop (arrow) of a snelled egg hook. (2) Pull the line to cinch up the yarn, then trim so the yarn is ¼ to ¾ inch (6 to 9 mm) long. The two-toned pattern sometimes catches fish when neither color alone draws a strike.

2. Make a fly from black, tan, or brown yarn. These flies don't resemble spawn at all, but rather natural foods, such as stonefly and mayfly nymphs. Also effective at times is blue yarn, though it resembles nothing steelhead or salmon would normally eat.

1. Cut lead-core line in several lengths from 18 inches (45 cm) to 6 feet (1.8 m) long. Form small loops on the end of each piece, just as you would on the end of a fly line.

2. Loop a section of lead core between your fly line and a 3-foot (0.9 m) mono leader. Use a short piece to sink a fly in shallow water, a longer one in deeper water.

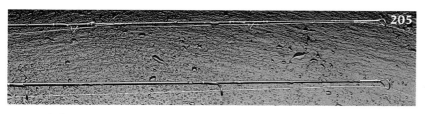

Use single-foot guides instead of the snake guides usually found on fly rods. The single-foots do a better job of holding the wet line away from the rod shaft. The result: your line zips through the guides with less drag.

PANFISH TIPS

207

Finesse Picky Perch

The motion and flash of a small jigging spoon gets a perch's attention. If the fish is aggressive, it will hit the spoon right away. A less active fish, however, watches the spoon but won't bite.

When finicky fish are giving you fits, try this rig. It catches these inactive perch and the aggressive ones at the same time, whether you're fishing open water or through the ice.

208

Detect Light-Biters

At times, crappies swim upward as they suck in a small jig, so you can't feel the strike. If you're using a regular bobber, it moves too little to notice. You can catch these fish, no matter how delicately they take your lure.

209

Outwit Fussy Crappies

In spring, you'll find crappies preparing to spawn in shallow water near cover such as brush or bulrushes. But often they don't feed much and shy away from most lures and baits.

Coax them into hitting by casting a lively minnow without a sinker. With no weight to hold it back, the minnow moves naturally and appeals even to the fussiest crappies.

Make a tandem rig by tying a barrel swivel to the line. Add 8 inches (20 cm) of 6-pound (2.7 kg) mono and tie a small jigging spoon on the end. Attach 6 inches (15 cm) of 4-pound (1.8 kg) mono to the swivel; add a small wet fly or nymph. Even perch with a full belly are curious; they'll move in to inspect the flashy spoon and may take a nip at the fly.

Use a European-style slip bobber (inset) on 2-pound-test (0.9 kg) mono to detect subtle takes. Tie on a $\frac{1}{64}$- or $\frac{1}{32}$-ounce (1 or 0.5 g) jig. Add enough split-shot above the jig that only about $\frac{1}{4}$ inch (6 mm) of the bobber sticks out of the water. Tiny European shot is best for the fine adjustment necessary. If a crappie swims upward as it sucks in the jig, taking some of the weight off the line, the super-sensitive bobber rises enough to clearly indicate a strike.

210

Modify Jigs for Papermouths

If you hook a crappie in the thin membrane around its mouth, the hook can tear out easily. Increase your chances of hooking a crappie in the tough tissue in the roof of the mouth.

Bend the hook of a crappie jig about 10 degrees past its original position. Now the hook is more likely to stick in the roof of the mouth than in the membrane.

211

Use Float Weight for Panfish Flies with Spinning Gear

One way to fish flies for panfish when using a spinning or spincast outfit is to use a clip-on bobber as a casting weight. Clip the bobber at both ends of the fishing line, about 2 feet (60 cm) up from the fly on the end of the line. Then cast and use a twitching retrieve to work the fly. The bobber can be removed to add a pinch-on or rubber-core weight to fish deep or to remove the fly to fish a lure.

212

A Little Leech Lasts Longer

Sunfish gobble up a small jig tipped with a piece of garden worm or nightcrawler. Trouble is, after one or two bites, the worm is gone. Here's a bait that's just as appealing but lasts much longer. Tip a $\frac{1}{32}$-ounce (0.5 g) jig with a $\frac{1}{2}$-inch (13 mm) piece of a leech, preferably from the narrow head end, where the flesh is toughest. The bait is small enough to catch nibblers, yet it will stay on the hook indefinitely.

213

No-Tangle Tandem Rig

Popper-and-nymph combos are great for bluegills in shallow water. The popper attracts the fish, but most of them, particularly the big ones, hit the nymph.

One common way of rigging flies in tandem is to cut your leader and join the pieces with a blood or barrel knot, leaving a tag end long enough for the dropper. But tying a dropper this way is time-consuming and the flies often tangle. Also, you need to tie up a new leader or cut the dropper off to go back to fishing one fly.

Here's a rig that's quick and easy to assemble, doesn't tangle, and is easy to take apart when you want to use a single fly.

Attach a small cork- or foam-bodied popper to a 6-foot (1.8 m) leader. Tie 2 feet (60 cm) of 4-pound (1.8 kg) mono to the bend of the popper hook with a clinch knot, then attach a size 12 weighted nymph. The popper makes a good strike indicator, disappearing when a fish takes the nymph.

214

Chum for Panfish

It's easier to bring panfish to you than for you to find them, especially when you're fishing through the ice. Borrow a tip from the saltwater angler's bag of tricks and try chumming. It works best for sunfish and perch, stirring up their competitive instincts so they feed more aggressively and keeping their interest so they stay around longer. Because fish must be able to see the chum from some distance away, chumming works best in clear water over a clean bottom, rather than in heavy cover.

215

Pennants for Panfish

Catching spawning bluegills or yellow perch is easy because you can see them in the shallows. But once the fish move to deeper water, they can be hard to locate. You need to bring the fish to you.

216

Read Depth through Bad Ice

In early winter, you can easily sound through the ice with a depth finder. But later in winter, snow, slush, and the air bubbles interfere with the signal, so you have to drill a new hole each time you want to take a reading. You can hear sound through the ice, even if the lake is covered by slush and snow.

Sound through recently drilled holes, where the ice is smooth and clear. Pour a little water on the ice, set the transducer in the puddle, and take a reading.

Drop a few BB-sized chunks of frozen shrimp down the hole. Once the fish move in, chum sparingly but often to keep them around. As you change bait, use your old bait for chum. It's important to drop the chum in the same spot each time. When fishing in open water, drop the chum next to a marker or other stationary object.

Drop a rope of colorful pennants (the kind car dealers use) in an area likely to hold bluegills or perch. A weight on one end of the pennant will keep them from drifting and a float on the other end will mark the spot. Leave the area for an hour or more. The bright flags attract these panfish and keep them in the area until you return. Fish around the flags with small jigs or live bait, either anchoring over the flags or casting from a short distance away.

217

Brush-Beater Crappie Jigs

Crappies often hang out in heavy brush and timber. No matter how carefully you work a jig through the branches, you snag up. Even if you don't lose the jig, you'll shake the branches as you try to rip free, usually spooking the fish.

One solution would be to put a mono-loop weedguard on your jig. Here's another way of rigging a snagfree crappie jig.

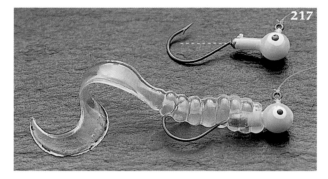

Bend the hook of a bare jig (top) downward about 20 degrees from the normal position (dotted line). Thread on a plastic grub so the hook point is barely exposed (bottom).

218

Another Type of Fishing Pier Rod Holder

A four-foot length of two-inch diameter plastic PVC pipe makes for a great fishing rod holder for fishing piers. The pipe is readily available in schedule 40 or heavier schedule 80 from home building supply, plumbing and hardware stores. Fasten the plastic pipe to a vertical rail support using two hook-end bungee cords to hold it in place vertically at two spots. Place the butt end of the fishing rod into the pipe end just as you would place a fishing rod into a surf fishing PVC sand spike. The bungee cords allow placing and removing the vertical support wherever and whenever you like, and will not harm the pier or interfere with other fishermen. These are easy and lightweight to carry in your wheeled pier fishing cart.

219

See Light Bites in the Dark

In midwinter, panfish sometimes mouth the bait so lightly you don't feel a thing. Or they grab the bait and swim up with it. Here's a way to detect these soft bites and set the hook.

Fish from a dark house or cover the windows of your fish house so you can see down the hole. In clear water, you'll be able to watch the fish take the bait. In deeper or murkier water, you probably won't be able to see the fish, but if you're using a light-colored bait, it disappear when a fish grabs it.

220

Super-Tough Perch Bait

The way yellow perch steal bait, you can spend more time baiting your hook than fishing. When you're jigging through the ice and fishing is hot, make a bait that attracts perch with smell, taste, and action and won't tear off the hook:

Scale the belly of a small perch and cut out an inch-long (2.5 cm) strip. Split one end of the meat to form two tails. Hook the other end of the strip on the jig.

221

Preserve Perch Eyes

Perch eyes make great bait for walleyes, saugers, and even perch. So, when you clean a mess of perch, poke out the eyes with your thumb and save them. But don't put the eyes in a freezer or they'll get mushy. Instead, put them in a small jar and fill it with saltwater. Keep the jar in the refrigerator until your next ice-fishing trip. Use an eye to tip a lure, or thread one on a plain hook and fish it on a 4-inch (10 cm) dropper beneath a small jigging spoon.

222

Light Up Ice-Fishing Holes

When ice fishing at night, it's tough to see a bobber. Most anglers set a lantern on the ice, but the bobber may be hard to see because of the shadow cast by the rim of the hole and when a fish pulls the bobber under, you can't see it at all. Try this trick to help you see better. It works with a light source as small as a candle or as large as a lantern.

Bore a hole in the ice between the holes you're fishing in, stopping just before the auger breaks through. Set a candle or lantern in the hole. Light travels through the ice to nearby holes, illuminating the bobbers from the side and below so they're plainly visible. Cover the hole on windy nights to keep the flame from blowing out, but be sure enough air gets in so the flame doesn't smother.

CATFISH TIPS

223

Keep Chicken Liver on the Hook

Chicken liver is a top channel cat bait, but liver won't stay on a hook if it gets warm and mushy. If you fish from the bank or a boat, keep the bait in a cooler. If you wade, pack the liver in a plastic bag and drop it in a canvas creel with an ice pack. The photos show three other tricks that help keep the bait on the hook:

224

Use Cotton Ball Strands for Better Dough Balls

Pull apart cotton balls and mix the fine strands with a dough ball to create a ball that will stay together better under water. The cotton strands give the dough texture and interlocking fibers to keep the dough ball on your hook intact.

225

Keep Baitfish on a Short Leash

Flathead catfish anglers often weight a big, frisky sunfish, sucker, or bullhead with a slip-sinker and put a sinker stop about 18 inches (46 cm) above the hook so the bait can move freely. But in the tangled timber big flatheads love, a baitfish on an 18-inch (46 cm) tether will hide in the wood or wrap your line around a snag.

Keep the baitfish close to the sinker by eliminating the sinker stop entirely or by placing a stop only a few inches (cm) up the line. Reel in the slack. If you want the baitfish to swim a little more, feed a few inches of line through the sinker. With the baitfish on such a short leash, a catfish can catch it easily.

226

Pre-Chum for Carp and Catfish

To increase your odds, pre-chum for carp and catfish. Set out some chum a few hours or a day before you plan to fish the area. Good chum for carp can be canned corn (scattered) and fist-size dough balls (use several). Once fishing the area, spread out more of the same chum and use the same for bait—several kernels of corn or a small dough ball on a hook. For catfish, spread out cut bait and use the same cut bait on your hook.

1. Impale the chicken liver on a number 8 or 10 treble hook, making sure each hook point pierces the bait. Whether the liver is firm or mushy, a treble hook holds it more securely than a single hook.

2. Wrap mushy liver in a patch of nylon mesh or stocking. The mesh lets odors escape yet keeps the bait from falling apart. Form a bag by gathering the edges of the fabric with the hook, twisting the hook to close the top and hooking the mesh again to keep the bag from opening up. Or tie the bag shut with thread before pushing a hook through it.

3. Mix chicken liver with Wheaties in a blender to form a thick paste. Mold the bait around a bait-holder treble hook to form a dough ball.

227

Line Release for Bank Fishing

When bottom fishing from shore with live bait, you should keep the line under a little tension so the wind or current doesn't carry it out. Yet line must pay out when a fish bites or it will drop the bait.

228

Steelheading for Catfish

Most catfishermen add a good-sized sinker to their line and let their bait rest motionless on the bottom of the river. In time, a catfish will usually find it. But enterprising anglers have discovered a quicker way to get a cat's attention.

Remove the front treble from a crankbait and substitute a leader and hook baited with a minnow, a gob of worms, chicken liver, or cut bait. Except that the baits are different, this is the same rig steelheaders use to fish along the bottom of a swift run.

Anchor below a riffle or wade out into it and let the rig trail in the deeper run downstream. You can move the bait from side to side simply by repositioning your rod. Reel in or let out line to move the bait farther upstream or downstream.

Even if the catfish are not in position to smell the bait, they can home in on the vibrations of the crankbait using their lateral line sense. Once they get close, they smell the bait and grab it, though occasionally a cat will hit the plug.

229

Keep Clam Meat on the Hook

Clams make good bait for catfish and many bottom-feeding saltwater fish, such as flounder and surfperch. The meat of a clam consists of the firm muscle mass, called the "foot," and some other tissue, which is softer. The foot is easy to keep on the hook; the other tissue is not. Most anglers use only the foot, but there's a way to make use of the soft meat as well.

Slip a loop of line under a matchstick held to the foregrip with a rubber band. The match keeps the line from drifting away, but releases the line when a fish hits. If the current or wind is strong, increase the friction on the loop by pulling the line in tighter to the rubber band. If there is little current, or if you feel that light-biting catfish are dropping the bait because they feel resistance, move the line farther from the rubber band. This way, the slightest tug pulls it free.

Wrap the soft meat with about 8 inches (20 cm) of thread, leaving the hook point exposed. The thread cuts into the meat, making a knot unnecessary.

230

Jigs for Cats

Few anglers think of jigs as catfish lures, but jig fishermen who target walleyes or bass in catfish waters catch plenty of cats by accident. It's not hard to understand why jigs catch so many catfish: They can easily be fished on the bottom, right where the catfish are.

Jigs tipped with live bait such as minnows, nightcrawlers, or leeches work best, although it's not unusual to catch catfish on plain bucktail, twister-tail, or rubber-legged jigs. Work the lure along the bottom in slow hops, just as you would for walleyes or bass.

231

Wild Baitfish Tame Cats

Veteran catfishermen know that baitfish caught from the river they're fishing are far superior to pond-reared baitfish purchased from the local bait shop.

Almost any kind of wild baitfish, including chubs, suckers, and sunfish, will work. The reason is simple: to baitfish that inhabit the river, catfish are natural enemies. When a hooked baitfish spots a cat, it struggles frantically to escape. The commotion arouses the cat's interest. A pond-reared baitfish, on the other hand, has never seen a catfish and has no reason to fear it.

232

Enhance Natural Odor

Flatheads, blues, and big channel cats are lazy; they'll eat a good-sized baitfish but usually won't go much out of their way to do it. You can make any baitfish more appealing to big cats by slowing it down so they can catch it more easily, and at the same time increasing the amount of scent it gives off.

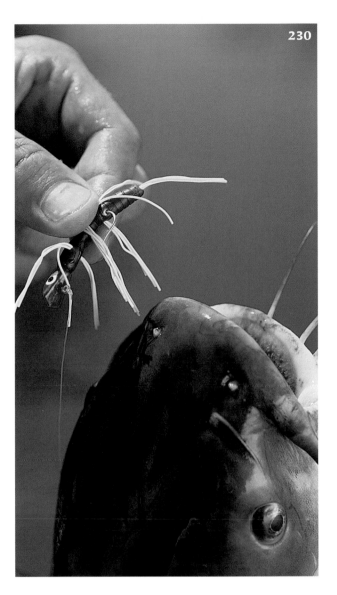

230

232

Trim part of the tail and pectoral fins before rigging the bait with a slip-sinker. The smell of fluids that seep from the cuts attract catfish. The bait will move frantically, but without normal fins won't be able to dodge a big cat.

233

Junkyard Slip-Sinkers

The debris-strewn bottoms of good catfish holes can gobble up a lot of sinkers. Cut your losses by making your own slip-sinkers out of otherwise worthless scrap.

234

Longer Lasting Scent

Catfish are drawn to some commercial and homemade scents, but many of thesm wash off after a few minutes in the water. To make the scent last longer, cut a piece of sponge about 1-inch (2.5 cm) square and bury a bait hook in it. Soak the sponge in scent. Fish the sponge in one spot or drift it slowly along the bottom. Reapply scent every half hour or so.

The sponge stays on the hook well and releases the scent slowly. Because it has a soft texture like real food, a catfish will pick it up and swim off, giving you time to set the hook.

235

Toughen-Up Bait

Almost any kind of dead minnows will catch channel cats, but dead bait softens up with use and tears off the hook. Here's a way to keep it on the hook much longer.

236

Feel Your Way around Snags

Big flatheads lie in deep holes filled with sunken timber. It's tough to know where to cast. Get too close to the wood and the sinker or hook will hang up. Stay too far away and the big cats won't find the bait. To place the bait properly, you need to figure out the precise location of the logs and limbs.

237

Use Peanut Butter for Catfish

Peanut better is an ideal food into which you can add other catfish baits for still fishing. It dissolves in time and in turn attracts catfish through a "chumming" technique. Baits to mix with peanut butter include bread, dough balls, cereal, flour, cornmeal, and blood baits. Mix until the result is stiff but moldable.

Tie a heavy washer, bolt, nut, or other scrap to a 12-inch (30 cm) piece of mono. Attach a barrel swivel to the other end. Slip the line from your rod through the free end of the swivel, and tie it to a second swivel. Run a short leader and bait hook off the second swivel. The "junkyard dropper" should be lighter than the main line. That way, if the scrap hangs up, the dropper breaks, sparing the rest of the rig.

Spread the minnows on a screen and let them dry in the sun for several hours. The screen lets both sides dry out and toughen up. Use the minnows as soon as they're dry or freeze them in a plastic bag to use later.

Fan-cast with a 1-ounce (28 g) bell sinker tied to the end of your line. Retrieve it along the bottom. The sinker seldom hangs up and you can feel it crawl over logs, limbs, brush, and rocks. Once you get a clear picture of the bottom, you can cast near snags but not into them.

238

Lift Baits above Snags

Years after a reservoir fills, a tangle of roots, limbs and logs remains on the lake bed, making it difficult to reach bottom-hugging fish without snagging the debris on the bottom. Here's how some southern catfish anglers solve the problem. The technique works in any snag-filled lake or slow-moving stream.

239

Cats Want Leeches Dead or Alive

Most anglers think of leeches as good bait for walleyes, but leeches also work well for a lot of other species, including channel cats.

Walleyes seldom bite on dead leeches, but channels don't seem to care whether they're dead or alive. In fact, when cats are off the bite, the rank smell of the dead leeches often stirs their interest.

Save your dead leeches; you may want to use them in combination with live ones or with some other type of live bait. Dead leeches keep for several days in cold water.

240

Remove Bullheads Fast

Bullheads often swallow the hook. Digging it out, even with a needlenose, is messy and time-consuming. Here's a quick way to get a bullhead off your line and get back to fishing.

Tie up several bait hooks on 1-foot (30 cm) leaders, each with a loop at the other end. Tie a snap to your fishing line and clip it to a leader loop. Bullheads aren't leader-shy and won't notice the snap. If one swallows the hook, unsnap the leader, clip on another, bait up, and return to fishing. Recover the hooks when you clean the fish.

Raise the bait off the bottom by pegging a 2- to 3-inch (5 to 7.6 cm) Styrofoam float about a foot up the leader (inset). The float lifts the hook and bait. The closer the float is to the hook, the higher the bait rides.

SALTWATER TIPS

241

Stand Sideways in Surf

Heavy breakers in the surf can knock you down, particularly the deeper you wade and fish. To minimize this possibility, turn sideways and jump up immediately prior to a breaker hitting you. By turning sideways, you minimize your surface area and the force of the breaker hitting you. By jumping, you minimize the effective height of the breaker, the force of the breaker hitting you, and the possibility of water running down your neck.

242

Make Inline Loops for Saltwater Bottom Rig

Use heavy line (40- to 50-pound-test [18 to 22.5 kg]) to make your own simple, single- or double-hook bottom rigs for saltwater fishing. Tie an inline dropper loop in the line. This is used to easily attach snelled hooks. A few inches (cm) farther down, tie on a large snap for adding a sinker to the rig. A few inches (cm) above the inline dropper loop, add a large swivel by which line can be tied to the rig. These rigs then allow adding a sinker for bottom fishing, a snelled baited hook to the loop and tying the rig to the main fishing line. You can also make these with two or more loops for snells by tying additional inline loops where desired and then adding the snap and swivel as outlined above.

243

Lure Polishing Materials

Ashes from campfires and cigarettes are idea for polishing metal tackle. Rub these ashes on metal spoons, trolling spoons, structure lures, tin squids, and spinner blades to get them shiny for attracting fish. When surf fishing, use beach sand for a quick metal polish.

244

Mark Transom or Gunwale for Measuring Fish

One easy way to measure fish for minimum size, maximum size, slot limits, and the like is to add a measuring tape to the transom or gunwale of your boat. Measuring tapes come in self-stick styles or plastic sticks that can be glued or screw-mounted. An alternative is to use permanent felt-tip markers on the transom or gunwale.

245

Use Umbrella Teaser Rigs for Maximum Saltwater Action

Umbrella rigs have a lot of little teasers and one main lure. They look like umbrella ribs (thus the name) and often consist of a series of soft plastic Sassy Shad-type lures with no hooks trailing from the ribs and a larger bucktail with a soft plastic tail from the center of the rig. The rig makes it look like a school of bait going through the water to attract fish.

246

Use Bridge Gaff

Using a bridge gaff is far easier if you are not the angler. If you are fighting a fish, have someone else handle the gaff if possible. If not, try to work the gaff with one hand while maneuvering the fish with the rod and other hand. To use a bridge gaff, first tie a loop (bowline, perfection loop knot, surgeon's loop) onto the end of the line and fasten it to the pier rail. Then drop the bridge gaff into the water near the fish. Make sure you do not get the fishing line and gaff rope tangled or twisted together. If possible, hold the bridge gaff slightly underwater and with your fishing rod, maneuver the fish over top of the gaff. With the fish over the gaff, raise the gaff sharply to catch the fish with the gaff points. Use the gaff line to bring the fish to the pier while reeling in excess line.

247

Don't Rest Rod on Rail

Never hold your rod against a rail or horizontal surface when fishing. Whether fishing from a pier, boat, bridge, or bank, holding a rod against a hard surface may cause it to break if a big fish hits suddenly. Also, if you are reeling in a big fish with the rod resting on a hard surface, a sudden surge by the fish can cause rod breakage. Hold the rod up and use a rod belt for support if necessary, but allow the rod to bend along its full length to cushion any shock.

248

Make Bridge Net

Bridge nets can be bought at some coastal shops, but you may have to make your own. To make a net, buy some heavy rod that you can bend into a circle or a length of metal electrical conduit that you can bend. To shape the rod, bend it around a bucket or similar large, round object to obtain the diameter desired. To bend hollow conduit, first fill the pipe with sand to prevent kinking it and then bend it around a bucket. You can also bend rod and conduit a little at a time in a vise. Remove the sand once the conduit is bent. The diameter should be similar to any net that you would use to land the fish sought. For most pier or bridge fishing, a net of about two to three feet (60 to 91 cm) diameter is best. Cut and fasten the two ends, using tape or wire over a rod or wood dowel ferrule in the two ends of conduit. Buy a replacement net bag and lash it to the frame by wrapping around the top net meshes and the frame. At three equidistant points around the frame, tie lines and then tie these lines of equal lengths to a welded ring. Tie a long length of ½-inch (13 mm) braided rope the ring to complete the bridge or pier net.

249

Use Rubber Band on Surf Reel Bail

Extreme force is used when casting a surf outfit to throw or cast a heavy lure or sinker far out into the surf. If your spinning reel does not have a "locked open" bail system, the bail can snap closed during the cast, ruining the cast and sometimes breaking off the lure or bait rig. To prevent this, loop-attach a rubber band to the bail.

250

Pier-Fishing Rod Protection

Pipe insulation that is split lengthwise to slip onto a water pipe is ideal for protecting rods when pier fishing. Piers have rails made of wood or metal and either material can damage a rod leaned against it. To avoid any damage, fit a 12-inch (30 cm) length of pipe insulation around the pipe or spread open and fit it to a wood rail for rod support and protection. Carry several such lengths in your gear bag when pier fishing. One 12-inch (30 cm) length for each rod used is best.

251

Use Bridge Net

As with a bridge gaff, a bridge net is easiest to use if one person uses the net while the angler handles the rod and fish. Tie the line of the bridge net to the rail of the bridge or pier. Drop the net to the water and hold the net a foot (30 cm) or so below the surface. Use the rod to maneuver the fish over the net. When the fish is completely over the net, raise the net sharply to secure the fish in the net and raise the net rapidly to the pier while at the same time retrieving any excess line. Two people are needed for this operation. Note that if the fish is too big to completely fit in the net, position the head and front of the body (the heavier part) of the fish over the net, and then raise the net.

1. On making a cast, open the bail and then loop the rubber band around the reel handle to prevent premature closure.

2. Once you complete the cast, pull the rubber band off of the handle and start retrieving or positioning the bait for still fishing. The rubber band does not interfere with retrieving line if you leave the rubber band in place

252

Use Stiff Rod, No-Stretch Line for Deep Jigging

Deep jigging saltwater lures, such as metal squids, spoons, and lead jigs, requires moving them up and down on or near the bottom to attract fish. Two things can make this difficult. One is a weak or flexible rod and the other is stretchy nylon line. For best result with deep jigging and to get the most action out of any bait or lure used, use a stiff rod that moves the lure when you work the rod. In addition, use a non-stretch line such as the gel-spun braided lines t0 move the lure rather than just stretching the line.

253

Add Reflective Tape to Lures

Carry a roll of reflective tape and a pair of scissors to add flash to lures while fishing. Self-stick reflective tape is available from many auto and general-purpose stores and is sold for safety reflective purposes. Cut the tape to size and shape and then stick to the lure with the lure dry. This trick works best on lures that lack extreme curved surfaces, such as some flat-side crankbaits, lipless rattle lures, spoons, spinner and spinnerbait blades, etc. A variety of colors plus silver and gold finishes are available. These make lures look more like baitfish.

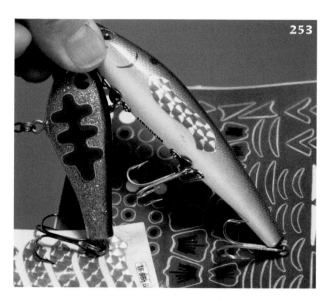

254

Make Bridge Gaff

When fishing from a pier or bridge, you will never be close enough to the fish to land it using a traditional net, gaff, or by swinging the fish onto the pier. You need a bridge gaff. To make a bridge gaff, buy four or six large-eyed hooks. These should be 10/0 or larger if possible. Clamp each hook in a vise and remove the barb with a file. Then fasten each hook around the circumference of a short length (6 to 8 inches [15 to 20 cm]) of metal conduit. Fasten the hooks by several holes straight through the conduit to attach the hooks with bolts and nuts through the eye of the hook and the conduit, one on each side of the conduit. Use several pairs of hooks to make a rig holding four or six hooks around the perimeter of the conduit. Use duct tape or wire to hold the hook shanks in proper position. Drill a hole straight through the top end of the conduit, run a bolt/nut through this hole, and add a chain snap link. Tie a ½-inch (13 mm) line to the snap link and make sure the line is long enough to reach the water from the pier.

255

Carry Clamp-On Rod Holder for Pier Fishing

Some piers have rod holders placed along the rail to hold rods. For those that do not have them, consider carrying a clamp-on boat-style rod holder that can be added to the rail of the pier to hold a rod for bait fishing while you use a second rod for casting lures or soaking bait. When buying such a clamp for this purpose, make sure it clamps onto the rail and can still hold the rod in the position desired. Some boat clamps are simple one-position-only, while others are very versatile for infinite adjustments and can be used on pier rails.

256

Release Deepwater Fish by Dropping Headfirst

Deepwater fish, such as tuna, false albacore, and others, have to constantly swim rapidly to keep alive. When caught and released, they should be handled as little as possible, kept a minimum amount of time out of the water, and released by dropping them forcefully headfirst. This forceful drop into the water forces water over their gills and gives them the best chance of survival.

Add Glitter to Lures

One way to make saltwater lures look more scaly and life-like is to add glitter to the body of a lure to simulate scales. The easy way to do this is to spray or brush them with a clear finish coat. While the clear finish coat is still wet, sprinkle the lure with glitter. To avoid wasting glitter, do this over a shoe box or similar container so you can salvage and reuse the excess. Glitter comes in many colors and several sizes to give you infinite choices. If done lightly, this does not hide the existing finish on your lures, but just adds a scale-like finish. Heavy thick finishes are particularly good for older lures that are losing some of their finish or looking a little old and dull in the water. Lots of glitter gives the lure a scaly, shad, or silversides minnow look which is ideal in saltwater.

258

Use Long Teaser Rod When Saltwater Fly Fishing

When fly fishing big gamefish from an offshore boat, teasers are used to attract the fish to the boat. These teasers are trolled from conventional rods. For fly fishing, it is best to use longer than normal teaser rods of about 7½ feet (2.2 m) rather than traditional 6-foot (1.8 m) trolling rods. The reason is that fish are teased to the boat where they are presented with the fly and a long rod makes it easier to jerk the teaser out of the boat wake when the fly is thrown in front of the fish.

259

Use the Sun to Your Advantage

When fishing the "flats" for bonefish, tarpon, or permit, you must be able to see the fish so you know where to cast. If the sun is in your eyes, glare on the water makes it hard to spot your quarry. Keep the sun behind you and wear polarized sunglasses.

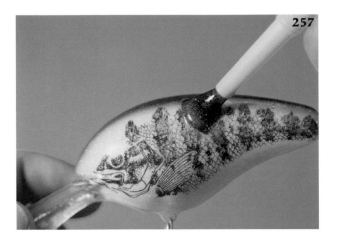

260

How to Unhook Birds

When saltwater casting to breaking fish, a line or lure catching a gull or tern is almost inevitable. Here is an easy way to unhook the bird: First, slowly and evenly reel in the bird, whether that bird is in the air or on the water. When it is close to the boat and able to be grabbed, have a fishing partner throw a large towel over the head of the bird while grabbing it. This calms the bird, lessens its fighting, and keeps you and your partners safe from biting and pecking bills. With one of you holding the bird to stabilize it, carefully follow the line or lure to determine how the bird was caught. Some birds get a wing tangled with the lure, others get hooked by the lure, and still others try to grab the lure, thinking it is bait. Untangle the line or unhook the bird. With the bird clear of the line, toss it into the air while still holding the towel.

261

Use Single Hooks for Bluefish

Toothy bluefish are often difficult to unhook when using crankbaits or other lures with treble hooks or more than one set of trebles. To solve this, use split-ring pliers to remove the treble hooks and replace with a one-size-larger single hook. This single hook still hooks and holds just as many bluefish but makes it both easier and safer when removing the hook from the fish.

262

Materials for Saltwater Boat Stripping Basket

Collapsible leaf baskets and clothes hampers make ideal stripping baskets when fly casting to breaking saltwater fish from a boat. Because they are collapsible, they can be folded and packed easily. If fishing in windy conditions, cover the bottom of the basket with sand or drop in some fishing weights.

263

Keep Skin with Strip Bait

There are several reasons for keeping the skin on strip bait. If trolling, the skin holds the meat of the strip together longer. It also usually has a white or bright shiny surface that looks like a baitfish to predators. If using it for cut bait, make sure you remove any large scales so you can run the hook easily through the meat and the skin when preparing the bait.

264

Make a Gaff for Landing Saltwater Fish

A simple, indestructible gaff for landing saltwater fish is easy to make with a length of 1-inch (2.5 cm) PVC pipe, a short length of dowel or broom handle, and a large hook. First, clamp the hook in a vise and use a file to remove the barb. Next, cut a 4-inch (10 cm) length of dowel or wood that will slip firmly into the PVC pipe. Draw an outline of the hook shank and eye on this dowel and then cut out recesses using a knife, chisel, drill, or motorized hobby tool. Insert the hook into the recess and drill an appropriate hole through the hook eye and wood dowel. Insert the wood dowel and hook into the bottom of the tubing and drill a hole through the tubing to match the holes in the wood. Insert a stainless steel round head bolt into through the tubing, wood dowel, hook eye, and out the other side of the tubing. Use a cap nut to secure it. If desired, wrap the handle end with cord and use a whip finish to complete it for better gripping.

265

Use Bright Line When Saltwater Trolling

Use bright-colored or fluorescent line when saltwater big-game trolling so you can see the position of the line. This is important for placing trolled lures in the right wake for maximum trolling efficiency and also when fighting a fish so you know the position of the fish.

266

Trim Flies with Barber Scissors

To thin out and feather tails or wings of saltwater flies, use barber thinning scissors with teeth like a comb that only cut some strands. These scissors are available at tool and equipment booths at sport, hobby, and fishing shows where they are much less expensive than from department stores or specialty barber shop supply houses. This technique can be used to trim saltwater nylon skirt jigs and trolling lures.

267

Make "J" Hook Tool for Easy Hook Removal

With a piece of ³⁄₃₂-inch (2.4 mm) steel rod available from a hardware or home workshop store, you can make an excellent tool for unhooking saltwater fish—especially those like bluefish that have teeth in the front end.

Obtain a piece of ³⁄₃₂-inch (2.4 mm) steel rod and a short, 6-inch (15 cm) length of 1-inch (2.5 cm) dowel. Square and threaded rod is available from home supply hardware stores, other rod at specialty and hobby shops. Cut the rod 1 foot (30 cm) long. In a vise, bend one end of the rod into a sharp "J". The "J" should have a bend of 1 inch (2.5 cm) or less, almost like an unsharpened miniature gaff hook. Drill an appropriate size hole through the center side of the dowel. One inch (2.5 cm) from this hole, drill a second hole part way through the dowel. Run the rod through the center-drilled hole. Place the rod in a vice and bend it with two sharp right-angle bends ½-inch and 1½ inches (1.3 and 3.8 cm) from the end. With a vise, clamp the rod and handle together so the ½-inch end of the rod rests in the blind hole.

If you want to get fancy, use a chisel to route a channel between the two holes so the rod is completely hidden in the handle. If desired, epoxy the parts together. Note that you may have to heat the rod with a torch to prevent it from breaking when making these sharp bends.

266

268

Use a Long Sand Spike

One advantage of a long sand spike (4 or 5 feet [1.2 to 1.5 m]) is that it holds the rod up higher and thus keeps the line above the breaking surf. Breaking waves catching the line drag sinkers when bait fishing and ultimately pull the bait toward shore. The disadvantage of a long sand spike is that there is much greater leverage to a fish taking the bait. Use a bait drag reel or a light drag setting so the rod is not pulled out of the long spike and into the beach sand.

269

Shorten Flies with Serrated Scissors

More and more streamer flies tied for saltwater are tied with synthetics including long-stranded nylon. As a result, these long wings are easily trimmed and made more lifelike with scissors. To trim the length of tails or wings on saltwater flies, use serrated-blade scissors. The serrated blades prevent slippery materials from sliding as you cut them.

270

Lure Choices for Tandem Rigs

To get the most hits and the most fish when using tandem rigs, mix the lures and colors of lures to give fish a choice. Thus, mix a crankbait with a small spoon, a jig with a spoon, a spoon with a spinner, etc. If using the same lures, use different colors for each of the tandem lures. Once you learn a distinct preference by the fish, you may want to switch to lures of that color or the lure type that the fish like that day.

271

Wet Towels Hold Fish

One way to easily hold a big saltwater fish by the lip to unhook it is to use a wet towel. Grabbing a pre-wetted towel is quicker and easier than trying to put on a cotton fishing glove for the same purpose. Use the towel to hold the fish by its lower lip using one hand while using the other hand, with or without pliers, to remove the hook or lure. Do this only with fish that have no teeth or very small teeth. It is ideal for striped bass, sea trout, snook, and sea bass, but not good for bluefish, barracuda, and similar species. When you are planning to keep fish, you can also use a towel to tail fish or grab them by the body.

272

Make a Chum Pot

A simple but effective chum pot can be made from a gallon-size (3.8 l) plastic mustard or mayonnaise jar. Wash the jar completely and drill holes through the center of the screw-on lid, opposite the jar sides below the lip, and all over the sides and bottom. Other than the ¼-inch (6 mm) holes in the lid and opposite sides of the lip, make these holes as large or small as desired to leak the chum used. An easy way to enlarge holes is with a reamer. To finish the chum pot, run a ¼-inch (6 mm) line such as parachute cord through the top and then through one side hole and around to the second side hole. This prevents loss of the lid and also allows for a rope handle for securing the pot.

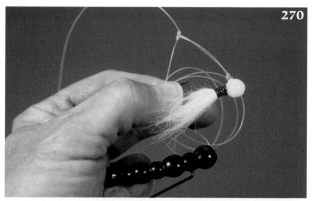

273

Use Chum Bomb of Bait and Sand

To chum deep, make chum bombs that are a mix of bait and sand. Make them fist-sized so you can drop them gently into the water to sink and then distribute chum on the bottom. To make these, prepare them before your boat leaves the dock or carry a bucket of sand with you to make them on the spot if needed.

274

Use Fluorescent or Bright Line in Surf Fishing

Use fluorescent or bright line in your surf fishing to be able to see the line. This allows you to adjust the line and rod height when fishing to prevent breakers from catching the line and pulling the bait inshore. It also helps when hooked to a fish by allowing you to see the line and position of the fish in relation to the beach, cuts, and sloughs.

275

Surf Rod Holders for Beach Buggy Bumper

A 6-inch (15 cm) or wider shelving or wood building board (2x6 or 2x10 [0.6 x 1.8 or .06 x 3 m]) works well as a beach buggy bumper base for PVC rod holders for surf rods. The board can be clamped onto the front bumper of a beach buggy and removed for street use after a surf trip.

276

Prevent Contact with Stingrays

Stingrays often feed on tropical flats where bonefishermen wade and cast. In addition, stingrays are almost impossible to see, since they hide on the bottom, disguised by sand over their wings. Step on one and it will try to drive its stinger into you. To prevent this, do not "walk" flats. Instead, slide your feet slowly along. By doing this, you scare any rays in front of you and they move away without harming you. In sliding your feet this way, do so very slowly so as to not create waves ahead of you that startle bonefish.

277

Using the "J" Hook Tool for Hook Removal

The "J" hook tool for removing hooks from fish is most handy when removing hooks from toothy fish such as Atlantic Coast bluefish, snappers, barracuda, etc. To use it, first grab the line and slide the hook of the tool down the line to the bend of the hook. If using a lure, grab the hook with the "J" hook of the tool. Then pull the line over and down while holding the "J" hook tool against the hook until the line is at a down angle and the fish is suspended by the barb on the hook point with the tool holding the hook by the bend. If the fish does not drop off, give the tool a shake to pull the fish off. Using this method, you can drop fish back into the water if undersized or for catch-and-release or drop the fish into an opened ice chest.

1. Various metal brackets and fittings such as "U" brackets, bolts with fender washers, "J" hooks, etc., are available for attaching the board to your beach buggy bumper.

2. Use a stout board as wide as your bumper or as wide as you wish the PVC holders. Use 2-foot (60 cm) lengths of 2-inch (5 cm) PVC tubing, with a "U" channel cut into the top to hold the arm of each spinning reel. Use "U" bolt brackets to clamp the PVC pipe vertically on the horizontal board. Two brackets are needed for each vertical PVC pipe. Make sure none of the rod handles drop below the bumper level where they can be damaged by street obstructions. If this is a problem, make one or more of the pipes longer than 2 feet (60 cm) or use a through-bolt at the bottom to prevent the rod butt from dropping through.

When to Kneel or Crouch

When tropical flats-fishing for bonefish, pods of bones zigzag, often coming close to where they can spot you. To prevent this and still have a possibility of getting off a cast, crouch or kneel low as you cast to prevent them from seeing you before you present the lure or fly to them.

279

Make a Rolling Tackle Box

A child's wood wagon often makes an ideal rolling tackle box for pier fishing in saltwater. Use the metal brackets (used for securing side slats) to hold wood boards that in turn support various components of your rig. Typical additions to the wagon can include a cooler for bait, bait board, separate cooler for lunch and drinks, tackle box for lures and rigs, bridge gaff or bridge net, vertical rod holders to hold pier rods, and a rack for bait and fillet knives along with pliers and dehookers. Such a mobile rig makes it easy to transport all your gear onto the pier for all your fishing needs for a day.

280

Prevent Beach Erosion, Sinking

Wading by standing in one spot when there is any current can cause the sand under your feet to erode. This happens when saltwater surf fishing with beach wave action and tides or when river fishing sandy bottoms. Ultimately, this will cause you to sink lower into the hole that is constantly being formed by this sand erosion. To prevent this, periodically move your position to a new spot. This might be only a foot or two (30 to 60 cm) away, as long as it is not part of the previously developing hole.

281

Hand Gaff with Rope Handle

Often it helps to have a hand gaff for landing big fish, but one that is easy to carry with you at all times and easy to pack when traveling. To make a simple gaff, use a large hook and file off the barb. Then use light braided rope or cord (such as parachute cord) for a handle. Knot the cord, run it through the eye of the hook, and then back through in the other direction. Knot the cord so the loop fits around your thumb and around the back of your hand when you hold the hook for gaffing. Do NOT run your hand through the loop—a large fish could pull you in. For obvious reasons, DO NOT use this on any toothy fish.

282

Belt Your Waders

Even with a waterproof parka when surf fishing, it is still possible for some water to get in your waders. Also, giant breakers or falling down markedly increase this possibility. To prevent this from becoming dangerous, wear a synthetic belt with smooth buckle over and around the wader to prevent water from going down inside the waders. Nylon belts are ideal for this. Make sure that it has a smooth, plastic Swedish-style snap buckle or two "D" or "O" rings for fastening.

283

Wash Rods after Saltwater Fishing

Rods are less susceptible to saltwater corrosion and damage than reels, but still must be cared for after each fishing trip. One good way to do this is to take the rods into the shower with you to wash the rods with a soapy washcloth. Make sure you move the collet nuts holding the movable reel hoods back and forth to remove any salt buildup in the threads. Rinse thoroughly and allow the rods to dry before storing them. This works for all types of rods used in saltwater—from light bay rods to heavy offshore billfish tackle.

281

284

Chum for Saltwater Fish

From a saltwater fishing boat, chum can be used in chum pots, chum bags, or frozen blocks. For best results, tie the chum container on a short line to a transom cleat so the chum container sloshes up and down with current waves and tide. That automatically distributes chum to keep fish coming to the boat. On a strong tide, do the same thing from a pier or dock. If the current or tide slows periodically, slosh the bag or container up and down to wash more water through it and to distribute chum.

You can do the same thing in freshwater boat fishing, but it is not be as effective since you don't have a tide to help distribute the chum. Before using chum in any situation, check to make sure it is legal.

285

Another Gaff for Landing Saltwater Fish

A second way to make a gaff for landing saltwater fishing is to use a wood handle or long, 1-inch (2.5 cm) dowel with a hook bolted to the lower end. To do this, first clamp the hook and file off the barb. Then decide on gaff length, cut to size, position the hook on the gaff handle, and drill through the wood. Use a stainless steel bolt and cap nut to secure the hook to the gaff. If desired, wrap the end of the gaff and the hook shank with cord to keep the gaff hook from sliding. Wrap the upper end with cord and whip finish it to make a handle.

286

Prevent Crabs from Stealing Bait

If losing baits to crabs when surf fishing, use floats on the end of leaders in fish finder rigs, two-hook or one-hook bottom rigs. The floats hold the bait up off of the bottom to prevent crabs from eating them. Most floats for this are available in bright colors to attract fish and can be found in surf shops.

287

Straighten Bite Leaders for Saltwater Fly, Spin Fishing

Bite leaders 1 to 2 feet (30 to 60 cm) long of 50- to 200-pound-test (22.5 to 90 kg) nylon monofilament are often used when fishing for toothy fish with fly, casting, and spinning tackle. To prepare these without coiling, use a board the length of the bite leader and wrap the nylon around the board, end to end. Then boil the board with the nylon line in a large pot, or if using 2-foot (60 cm) lengths, in a long fish-poaching pan. After boiling, rapidly cool the nylon and board in a tub of cold water. Allow to cool completely. Use heavy, serrated-blade scissors to cut the bite leader lengths from the board for use when fishing.

288

Make Sand Spike to Hold Surf Rods

Sand spikes are used to stick into the beach sand
and hold surf rods while bait fishing. An easy way
to make a sand spike for fishing the surf is to use
PVC pipe. You can get PVC pipe in 1½- and 2-inch
diameters (3.8 and 5 cm) from any hardware or
home supply store. Schedule 40 is the best wall
thickness; schedule 80 is thicker than you need.
Make the sand spikes by cutting the PVC pipe at
a 30-degree angle to create a point to stick easily
into the sand. That also allows you to make several
spikes from one 10-foot (3 m) length (often the
way it is sold) with the only waste perhaps a small
cut at the end. The best sand spike lengths are
about 3 feet (2.7 m) long, although you can make
them any length. If desired, cut a notch into the
upper end of the spike into which to position the
arm of the spinning reel.

289

Bite Leader Storage

To store long nylon bite leaders (50- to 200-
pound-test [22.5 to 90 kg]) for fishing, use a
length of ½-inch (13 mm) PVC or CPVC plastic
water pipe. Glue a PVC cap to one end and use
a second as a slip fit onto the end to retrieve
lengths of the bite leader. Mark the side of the
pipe with the pound test of the bite leader and
use different PVC sleeves if using more than one
size of bite leader.

Protect Gaff Points with Plastic Hose

To protect both gaffs and people, gaffs should have
a protector that slips over the point. If your gaff
lacks this, you can make one from a short length of
vinyl hose. Use a length the inside diameter of the
gaff point. Cut the hose to length so it slips onto
the gaff point to the hilt and also is long enough to
slip into the point for protection. Slide one end of
the tubing into the gaff, then penetrate the side of
the tubing about 2 inches (5 cm) into the tubing.
Slide the tubing to the hilt of the gaff and secure
with tape if necessary. Use the other end of the
tubing to protect the point and slip off the point
when gaffing a fish.

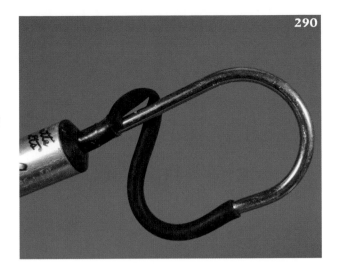

291

Saltwater Vinyl-Skirt Trolling Lures

Use 50- to 100-pound-test (22.5 to 45 kg) nylon monofilament, solid wire, or braided wire as the core
for making simple vinyl skirt saltwater trolling lures. You need trolling skirts, mono or wire, nesting tri-
beads or snowflake beads, hooks, and egg sinkers. Begin by securing (knot, leader-sleeve or twist-in solid
wire) a hook to the core line. Then add plastic tri-beads or snowflake beads. When the core leader length
is long enough, add an egg sinker of appropriate size, then add the vinyl skirt and make a loop at the
end of the core leader. The lure is ready to fish by trolling behind a boat. Any color or size lures can be
made this way.

292

Wash Tackle after Saltwater Trips

For best results when fishing with terminal tackle, lures, flies, or using different hooks, keep all fished-
with tackle separate from unused tackle. That way, you won't mix the two and possibly cause saltwater
corrosion in your tackle box. One simple strategy is to keep all fished lures, rigs, and flies in a separate
container, such as a plastic storage box or large zipper-seal plastic bag. That way, you can wash these
items when finished fishing and dry them before returning them to your tackle or fly containers. Wash
in soapy water, scrub with an old toothbrush if necessary, rinse thoroughly, and then lay out to dry. Do
not return any item to your tackle storage until everything is completely dry.

Chapter 3

MAKING & MODIFYING LURES

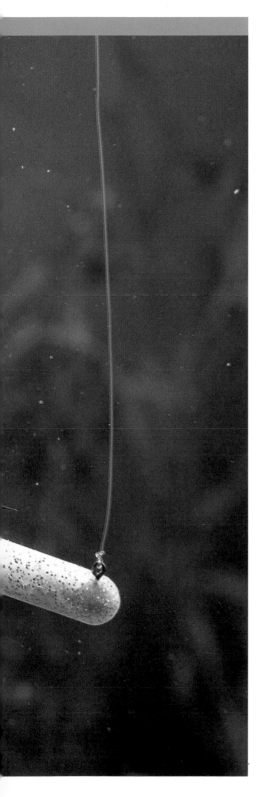

Most lures are great just as they come out of the tackle shop, and catch lots of fish. But you can always improve lures or make new ones by following a few simple tips and tricks.

These can be as simple as modifying a Texas worm rig or coloring a lure with a felt-tip marker. They can also be more complex, such as repairing soft plastics with a flame or making chum pots for deep water bait fishing.

They are all easy to do, and will help you take home your share of the catch.

293

Make Mini Chum Pot from Film Can

Before we all go completely digital, collect some film cans from a photographer friend or photo store. You can use these film cans for mini chum pots when bottom fishing freshwater or saltwater. Punch or drill a small hole in the center of both the top and bottom. Then drill or punch holes all along the sides. Make the hole the sizes needed for the chum to be used to leak out. Keep several of these mini chum pots on hand for deep water bait fishing.

294

Use Mini Chum Pots for Deep Bait Fishing

To use a mini chum pot, run the line through the top and bottom hole of the chum pot, then add a hook, sinker, and any other rigging you wish. If you wish to keep the chum pot above the baited hook, add a split shot above and below the chum pot several inches (cm) to a foot (30 cm) above the baited hook. Once rigged, add the chum to the mini-pot and fasten the lid. Do not add the chum first, otherwise you will not be able to run the line through the pot.

295

Use Texposed Rig if Fish Strike Lightly

To rig a weedless worm for fish that are only striking lightly, use the modified Texas rig, often called a Texposed rig. In this, first rig the worm and hook just as you would a regular Texas rig. The main difference is that as you bury the hook, bury it deep and close to the surface of the opposite side of the worm. Then expose the hook point and finish by lightly burying the point end back into the worm. The hook point is protected, but with the slightest strike, the point pops out to hook the bass.

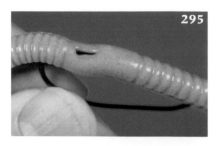

296

An Improved Texas Rig

With a regular Texas-rigged worm, you miss strikes because fish grab the worm behind the hook. But if you rig the plastic worm as shown below, the hook is far enough back to catch short-strikers. The sinkers are inside the worm, offering several other advantages:

They keep the worm from sliding down the shank when you set the hook; they won't separate from the worm, so pegging is unnecessary; and they're covered by soft plastic, so bass hang onto the worm longer.

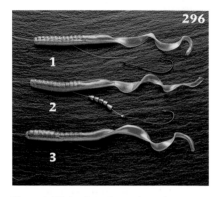

Thread (1) the line through a plastic worm so it comes out about one-fourth of the way back. Simply use the hook as a needle. (2) Thread several $1/64$- or $1/32$-ounce (1 or 0.5 g) bullet sinkers onto the line nose first and tie on the hook. (3) Draw the sinkers and the eye of the hook into the worm by pulling on the line; push the hook into the worm so the point barely protrudes. The worm should hang straight so it doesn't twist your line.

297

Add Chamois to Spoon for Trailer

One way to make easy trailers for saltwater spoons and other lures is to use an inexpensive leather chamois such as is sold in auto supply shops for polishing cars. This also allows you to make large long trailers as are used in saltwater and trailer strips that do not go bad as do bait strips. Chamois is leather made from a chamois (a small goat-like animal) or from deer, goat, or sheep. It stays soft and flexible even after becoming wet, which makes it ideal for trailers. Cut the chamois into a long bait-like strip or into a long thin "V" or similar shape. Add it to single hook lures or as a trailer on the rear or multi-hook lures. You can also color the fawn-colored chamois with clothing dye or by marking it with permanent felt tip markers.

298

Fizzing for Fish

When fish are fussy, even the slow movement of a plastic worm or soft-plastic tube jig may not get them to strike. The photo shows an unusual presentation that can really pay off.

Crumble an Alka-Seltzer tablet and slide the chunks in the rear of a soft-plastic tube jig. Stuff cotton in the tube to hold the Alka-Seltzer in place. Fish the lure slowly. As water soaks through the cotton, the Alka-Seltzer begins to fizz. The bubbles that stream from the rear of the jig attract fish and often trigger a strike. This is a proven tactic for largemouth bass, but don't hesitate to try it on other species, as well.

299

Make Tail-Hook Tool for Worm Rigging Variations

A tool for making a lot of hook rigging variations is easy to make. Begin by getting a long upholstery needle and insert the needle end into a short handle of a wood dowel. If necessary, drill a tiny hole in the handle and glue the needle in place. That way, you can run the needle through the worm tail first, insert the mono in the needle eye, and pull back through the worm to tie on the hook. This also allows you to rig hooks in any part of any soft plastic lure.

300

Use Nail Polish for Lure Touch-Up

For quick in-the-field touch-up paint jobs on lures, try fingernail polish. Many colors are available, including both opaque and translucent along with glitter finishes. The nail polish dries quickly to allow you to go back to fishing within a few minutes of restoring a lure.

301

Spinning Worms for Bass

Most plastic worm fishermen bump the lure slowly along the bottom. It's a deadly but very slow method. But when bass are scattered in the shallows, you may catch more fish by using a faster retrieve to cover more water. Here are two ways to rig a worm so it can be worked rapidly across the surface. Because the worms are rigged crooked, they spin on the retrieve, drawing explosive strikes.

Thread a 6-inch (15 cm) worm on a barbed-shank worm hook so half the bend is covered. Add a swivel above the hook to prevent line twist. Slide the end of the worm over the hook eye; poke a piece of toothpick or mono through the eye to keep the worm in place. The worm has a kink in it so it springs when reeled in. Make a weedless version by threading the worm on a worm hook and twisting it a quarter turn before reinserting the hook Texas style.

302

Revive Pork Baits

Dried-out pork baits can often be revived with the brine from a bottle of pork rind. Place the dried pork chunk or strip into the brine for a few hours or more. In time, most dried pork absorbs enough brine to be soft, flexible, and usable again.

303

More Spinnerbait Rattle

An easy way to add more noise to any spinnerbait is to use electrician's tape to secure a plastic, glass, or metal rattle onto the lower arm of the lure. You can even bunch up two or three rattles this way to make more noise, or mix glass, plastic, and metal for different sounds. You can add color to the lure with plastic electrician's tape.

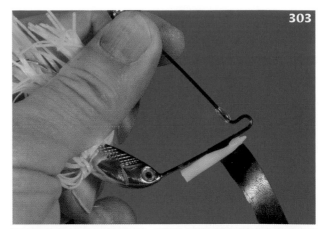

304

Prevent Fly Line Tangles

Loose fly line tangles around practically everything in a boat, causing lots of aggravation when you're trying to cast. Here's an easy way to keep the line from wrapping around such items as outboard tillers, gas cans, and tackle boxes: Spread a 4-by-6-foot (1.2 to 1.8 m) minnow seine over all the objects that can snag your line. The weights and floats on the edges will hold the netting down so it doesn't blow around.

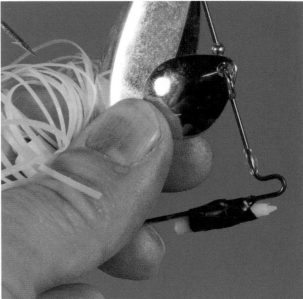

305

Stabilize Tail-Hooked Soft Plastic Worms

If fishing a tail-hooked soft plastic worm in snaggy water, the worm might snag on brush and slide down on the line to make the worm unattractive. In these cases, adjust the worm after tying on the hook. Slide the worm down on the line, then add a small split ring by inserting the doubled line through and around the split ring to make a cinch knot. Then carefully pull the worm up to bury the split ring in the head of the worm. Secure by running a toothpick through the worm head and the buried split ring. Clip or break off the exposed toothpick ends.

306

Add Plastic Eyes

To make lures more lifelike and attractive to fish, buy plastic eyes in a craft or art store and glue them onto spinner blades and spoons blades. Eyes of many sizes are available. On spoons, glue both eyes to the outside (convex side) of the blade. You can also do this with spinner blades or you can glue one eye on each side (one each on convex and concave sides) of these rotating blades. The eye on each side makes for an eye-catching effect as the blade rotates and catches the attention of fish. For blade baits, glue one eye on each side of these weighted, vibrating metal lures. The best way to glue these is to thoroughly clean the blade and use epoxy to glue the eyes in place.

307

Mow Weeds with a Spinnerbait

Thick submerged weeds, such as hydrilla and coontail, cling to a spinnerbait and ruin its action. Here's a clever way to modify a spinnerbait so you can work it through the weeds with fewer hang-ups. Select a spinnerbait with a heavy brass willowleaf blade and an attachment eye that is not twisted to form a loop in the wire. If the lure has a twisted eye, a clevis, or beads, it catches more weeds on the retrieve.

File the leading edges of the blade and hone them until they're razor sharp. Now the blade will cut through the weeds so they can't foul the lure.

308

Use Loop Knot in Heavy Line for Lure Action

For maximum action in a lure when fishing with a heavy line, do not use a tight knot such as an improved clinch knot or Palomar. Instead, use a loop knot such as a Homer Rhode loop knot or Rapala loop knot. The advantage of a loop knot in heavy line is that the lure or hooked bait has maximum action. Using a tight knot reduces the possibility of action and minimizes movement of a lipped swimming lure.

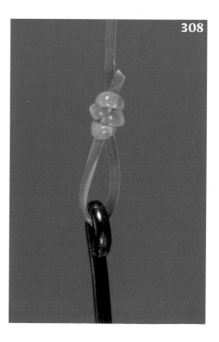

309

Divide Jig Weedguard into "V" for More Protection

Brush-style weedguards in a tight bundle on jigs can still allow a hook point to get snagged in very weedy situations. To prevent this, divide the brush guard with your fingers and then place an index finger between the two bundles. Push down to the base of the jig head. Work your finger side to side so the brush guard is spread out to the sides, like the outrigger on a boat. This provides more side-to-side protection to the lure point and prevents the jig from getting snagged.

310

Depth Control for Spinnerbaits

How deep a spinnerbait runs depends on how fast you retrieve it. The slower you reel, the deeper it tracks.

But changing speeds to run at the right depth may reduce the number of strikes you get. You can change the running depth of a spinnerbait without altering the speed.

Bend the arm from its normal position (dotted line) to widen the angle and make the lure run shallower. To fish deeper, bend the arm the other way.

311

Pliable Pegs

Some anglers peg their worms by pushing a toothpick through the hook eye to keep the worm from sliding down the hook. But when you pull through weeds or set the hook on a short-striking fish, you may tear the worm off the toothpick. You want to keep the worm from ripping off so easily.

312

Make Your Own "Bleeding" Bait and Worm Hooks

You can make your own bleeding bait hooks by painting a hook with powder paint. Powder paint is sold for painting metal lures. It is basically a powder pigment designed for use with an electrostatic charge for painting appliances, cars, and similar metal products. It is also used to paint metal objects by dipping a heated object into the pigment. To use, heat the hook bend and shank in a flame until hot. Avoid heating and affecting the temper of the hook point and also use only minimal heat. Then dip the hook into the powder paint to color it. Shake off any excess powder for use the next time. If the hook is not hot enough, the paint will not stick and requires subsequent heating and dipping. You can do this with any color from these paints that are available from tackle shops and catalog houses.

Peg the worm with a short piece of 80-pound-test (36 kg) mono; trim the ends flush with the worm. The mono has more give than a toothpick, so when you jerk, the mono bends instead of ripping through the worm.

313

Test Hook Sharpness with Thumbnail

Once a hook is sharp—or you think that it is sharp—test it. An easy way to do this is to hold the hook with the point touching your thumbnail. Do not use any pressure on the hook, but pull on the hook and see if it catches on your thumbnail. If it catches easily, it is sharp. If it does not, it needs further sharpening.

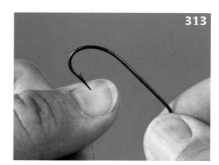

314

Metal Tubes for Casting Spoons

With a hacksaw, vise, and a little time, you can make bunch of inexpensive casting and deep jigging spoons. Buy or get cooper, brass, chromed (bathroom), or galvanized tubing. Place in a vise and cut repeatedly at an angle to make lengths of angled tubing lures. Drill a ⅛-inch (3 mm) hole in each end. Add a split ring and treble or single hook to one end and a split ring to the other for a line tie. These lures in different metallic finishes spin and jerk, twist, and wobble for good action and lots of strikes from big fish.

1. To insert the marabou stem into the tail of the worm, use a larger-eye needle and thread the marabou or feather stem through the eye, then run the needle through the end of the tail.

315

Add Marabou to Tail of Plastic Worm

To add more action to a plastic worm, add a marabou tail to the worm. You can buy marabou or fluffy feathers from any fly or fly tying shop and from most craft stores.

316

Use Red Trailer Hooks for More Attraction

Red trailer and stinger hooks can resemble blood oozing from a baitfish and thus serve as an attractant to fish. Where possible, use these red hooks on all your stinger or trailer hook rigs for lures.

2. When the tail is positioned properly, hold the marabou tail ends and pull out the needle. To keep the feathers from falling out of the worm, add a small drop of CA glue to the stem just before you pull it into the worm and immediately remove the needle so the feather does not stick to it. If desired, you can do the same thing to add "legs" or "fins" to any soft plastic lure or worm.

317

Different Spinnerbait Action

For different action with a spinnerbait, use your fingers or pliers to slightly bend the blade to make it spin faster, slower, or differently as the blade turns through the water. Try the lure each time you make a bend so as to get the action, noise and spin rate desired.

318

Another Pork Chunk Modification

Inserts into a pork chunk can also add to its attractiveness and make it more attractive to bass and other gamefish.

319

Hard-to-Throw Buzzbaits

Buzzbaits stir up plenty of action in heavy cover, but a leaping bass can easily throw the heavy, long-bodied lure. As the bass shakes its head, the lure flops back and forth, twisting the hook, enlarging the hole in the fish's mouth, and allowing the hook to back out. Doctor the buzzbait so it's considerably harder for a bass to throw.

320

Add Glitter to Pork Chunks, Strips

Some pork strips and chunks are available with glitter in the brine solution that sticks to the pork to make it more attractive in the water. To get the same effect with a bottle of pork lacking glitter, buy glitter from a craft, art, or hobby shop and add it to the brine. After restoring the cap, shake the jar to distribute the glitter through and coat all the contained pork. With this trick, you can use any color glitter or glitter that comes in mixed colors. You also have a choice of glitter sizes.

Use a large upholstery needle to run yarn through the pork chunk. You can do this side-to-side or top to bottom. Use one or more strips of yarn. The favorite color for this is red, but any color or type of yarn is possible. Vary the length of the yarn or use long strips of yarn and cut back as desired when fishing.

Modify the buzzbait by snipping the shaft, forming eyes in the wire, and joining them with a split ring. It's important to form the eyes by bending the wire up (arrows) so the ends are behind the prop arm, where they won't catch weeds. The hook of this pointed buzzbait moves independently of the heavy blade, so bass have a hard time shaking it loose.

321

Riffling Hitch Changes Action

A riffling hitch, developed by Atlantic salmon
fly fishermen, works well with any streamer fly
retrieved on the surface. It makes a fly run at an
angle to the angler and also creates a splashy,
injured minnow look.

322

Repair Soft Lures with Flame, Heat

Use a flame from an alcohol lamp, cigarette
lighter, or grill starter as a welding tool to repair
soft plastic lures. The best of these is an alcohol
lamp or similar flame that sits alone so you can
use both hands. To repair soft plastic lures with
tears and holes, hold the tear or damaged area
close to the flame to just barely melt the plastic
and cause it to float and flow with the plastic body
to repair any damage. Allow to cool slightly before
using. If making a bunch of repairs, it helps to
keep a bowl of water close by into which to dump
the lures to cool them.

323

Two-Way Trailer

When spinnerbait anglers add a trailer hook to
catch short-striking fish, they push it over the
main hook point up. This system works fine in
heavy cover. The trailer doesn't snag many weeds
because the hook point is protected.But when
you're working open water, try rigging the trailer
point down. With one hook pointing up and the
other pointing down, your hooking percentage
will increase.

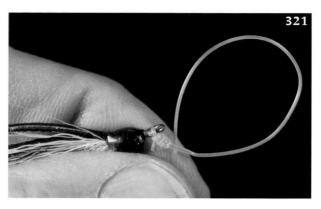

1. Tie the leader tippet to the fly hook eye, using an
improved clinch knot.

2. Pull the knot back toward the head of the fly, coil the
tippet, and place the coil over the head of the fly. Add a
second identical coil and the fly is ready to fish. Note that
you can place the tippet leading from this coil on either side
of the fly, depending upon where you are fishing and how
you want the fly presented and retrieved.

324

Tuning Spinner Blades

Commercial spinnerbaits and in-line spinners have cupped blades that start turning easily and spin rapidly. But sometimes fish don't respond to the vibrations of a standard blade. Modify your spinner blades so they make a different sound, which may be more appealing1

325

Homemade Trailer Hooks

Many commercially made trailer hooks have vinyl-coated eyes to hold them firmly on the bend of the main hook. Otherwise, the trailer would flop around or fall off entirely.

If you can't find trailer hooks with vinyl-coated eyes or if they're not available in the style or size you want, you can easily make your own using almost any long-shanked hook with a large straight eye.

326

Get Splashing, Gurgling Action

One way to make a surface splashing lure with a different action is to cut off the front half of the lip on a shallow-running crankbait. Do this only with shallow running lures that have the lip set an angle to the body, not parallel or close to parallel to it as with deep-diving baits. Use the cutting part of fishing pliers to do this in the field, or use a fine-tooth hacksaw blade if preparing lures at home. The result is a lure that will run very shallow and splash on the surface or alternately run just under the surface to mimic an injured minnow, splashing bait. It makes for a different look than most lures and one that will attract any feeding predator.

Flatten the blade on a rock or anvil. The flat blade creates more resistance and a slower, more throbbing beat than the original.

Coat the eye of the hook with a waterproof, flexible adhesive (the kind you would use to patch waders). Or dip the eye in the liquid vinyl sold in hardware stores to coat and insulate tool handles. When the coating dries, push the trailer hook onto the main hook.

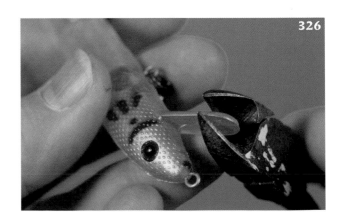

327

Snag-Resistant Snake Plugs

Fish can't resist the wild action of a jointed minnow plug. But it's almost impossible to use these lures in weedy or brushy cover because they foul immediately.

Make a jointed minnow plug more weedless while adding the enticing swimming action of a plastic worm.

328

Tail-Hook Plastic Worms

Sometimes, bass or other gamefish miss hooks when a worm is hooked at the head end using a Texas or Carolina rig. One way to solve this problem and hook more fish is to hook the worm at or near the tail. Usually this works best with a thick-bodied worm but, with care, it works with any worm or soft plastic. Use a long upholstery needle and run your monofilament line through the eye. Then thread the needle through the worm starting at the head end and coming out of the worm about two to three inches from the tail. Remove the line from the needle and tie it to a hook. Then pull the line through the worm to bury the hook shank into the body of the worm for an exposed hook rig. If using a Texas-style rig, bury the end of the shank in the worm and then rotate the worm to bury the hook point in the worm body.

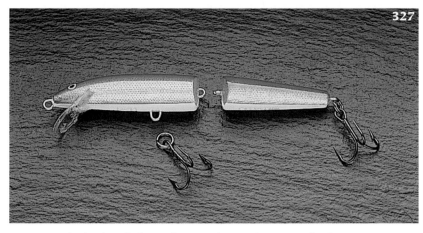

1. Remove the back end of a medium-sized jointed minnow plug by cutting or opening the rear eye; take off the front treble and split ring.

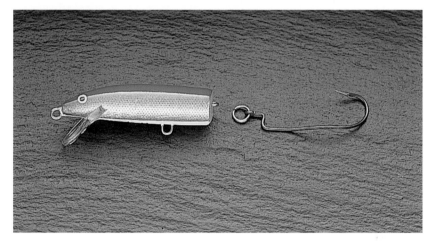

2. Twist the eye on the front section so it is horizontal. Slide a split ring onto a 3/0 worm hook, then join the split ring to the plug so the hook rides point up.

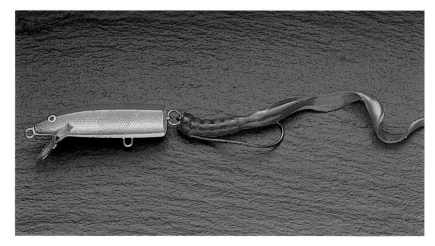

3. Rig a 4-inch (10 cm) plastic worm on the hook Texas style. Fish the lure in pads, stumps, and trees, retrieving it steadily so it swims at or near the surface like a snake. When a fish hits, pause a second before setting the hook.

329

Add Keel Weight or Pinch-On Sinker to Lower Wire on Spinnerbaits

To add weight for deeper fishing of any spinnerbait, add a pinch-on sinker to the lower arm. Use a regular screwdriver to slightly open up the slot on the pinch-on sinker, then slide it onto the lower arm of the spinnerbait and pinch the sinker closed with pliers or fold over the tag end arms. If you wish to keep this permanent, paint the weight for more color.

330

Use Wire "Guide" for Sensitive Ice Fishing Pick-Up

To make a sensitive gauge for light pick-ups of fish when ice fishing, take an 8-inch (20.3 cm) length of 50-pound (22.5 kg) twisted (braided) wire and bend to make a small ring or line guide on one end. Tape the straight end to the end of the rod with the wire extended in front of the tip top or end guide. Run the line through this wire guide so with a still-fished rod, any light touch to a bait causes the wire to bend and wiggle, alerting you to a hit.

331

Mark Lures with Felt Tip Markers

Carry some bright permanent felt tip markers to mark your fishing lures in the field. Mark the lure when it is dry or dry it with a terry rag before trying to mark it. With markers, you can color the whole lure or make patterns, stripes, or dots to attract fish. This is an easy technique with crankbaits, top water lures, spoons, spinner blades, jig heads, and trolling spoons. This allows dressing up lures with faded colors or adding high-contrast lines, which work for greater visibility and attractiveness.

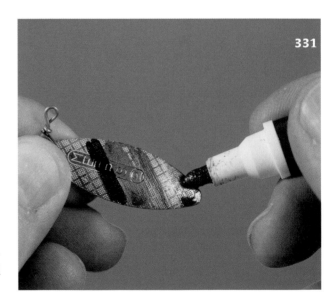

332

Better Sinking Flies

Most fly tiers wrap lead wire around the hook shank of streamers and nymphs to make them run deeper but the lead wire causes the fly to sink horizontally. The water resistance against the entire length of the fly minimizes the sink rate. Also, the fly doesn't have much action. Here's a better way to weight flies.

Instead of wrapping lead on the hook, tie the fly on a bare jig. Flies tied on jig hooks have an appealing jigging action and sink head first, so they get down to the fish faster. Because they ride point up, they don't snag as often.

For best casting, use a jig no larger than ½2 ounce (1 g). But jigs this size usually have hooks too small for good-sized fish. To get the hook you want, you can mold your own jigs. Or use bigger jigs and shave off some lead with a file or old knife. Another solution is to buy plain jug hooks (without the lead) and squeeze on a split-shot of the desired weight.

333

Double-Skirted Spinnerbaits

Most spinnerbaits and buzzbaits have rubber skirts to add action, color, and a full silhouette to the lure. Sometimes anglers want to add yet another skirt to make the lure appear larger or to add another color or to slow the sink rate to keep the lure near the surface on the retrieve. But with a second skirt, bass may strike short. You can add a skirt without reducing your hooking percentage:

Make a double-skirted spinnerbait by sliding a skirt over a trailer hook. Then push the main hook through the skirt's rubber sleeve and the eye of the trailer. Push the trailer into place on the bend of the main hook.

334

Use CA Glue to Fasten Plastic Worm to Hook

Some special glues are sold for gluing a plastic lure to a hook, but you can use any cyanoacrylate (CA) glue. These glues are quick drying but do have the disadvantage of gluing your fingers if you are sloppy. Use carefully and add just a drop of glue to the hook shank before burying the hook in the body of a worm in a Texas rig or exposed hook rig. This tip particularly helps to prevent missed fish by largemouth and smallmouth that do not get a good grip on the worm or have to mouth it again, giving you time to set the hook without a worm sliding down the hook.

335

Increase Gap on Jig Hooks

Use pliers to increase the gap on jig hooks for better, easier, and faster hooking of fish. Often as little as a 5- or 10-degree increase in point position does not affect jig performance but can increase hooking ability. Do this carefully and wear safety goggles, since a brittle hook can snap.

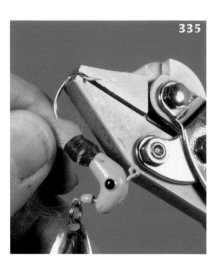

336

Easy Jig Eyes

Many anglers are convinced that eyes make lures more effective. But the eyes are tough to paint on neatly if you don't know how.

337

Modify Spoons for Different Speeds

Lightweight trolling spoons have good action within a narrow range of speed. Troll too fast and they spin, twisting your line; too slow and they drag through the water without much wobble at all. You can find the best speed by trolling your spoon next to the boat and varying your speed until it wobbles just right. But a problem arises when you want to run that spoon with other lures that troll best at different speeds. Make the spoon work at higher or lower speeds so you can use it with these other lures.

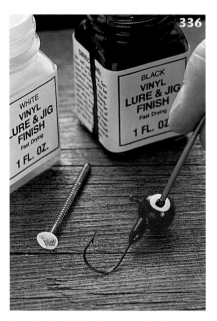

Dip the head of a large nail in light-colored paint and dab it on the lure to form the eye. Let it dry. Dip a finishing nail in dark paint to make the pupil.

338

Add Flash

A long upholstery needle is handy for adding flash to clear or very transparent soft plastic shrimp and saltwater baitfish. This added flash in a saltwater soft plastic can work as an added visual attractant to draw fish that might otherwise ignore a lure. Mylar or other flash material used by fly tiers works well. You can also use Mylar icicles on sale after Christmas or similar decorations after Halloween. Use a needle-eye threader to run a few strands of this material into the eye of a long upholstery needle. Then carefully run the needle through the center of the soft plastic lure, starting at the head end and working to the tail. Pull the needle through with the Mylar or flash and then cut or pull the flash material out of the needle at the end of the worm. If you do a lot of this, make it easy by using a fine file to cut a notch in the lower part of the eye to instantly slide flash into the needle eye.

339

Make Spinnerbait Weedless with Rubber Band

It is easy to make a spinnerbait weedless with a small rubber band. Run the rubber band through the eye of the spinnerbait, then run the rubber band through itself and pull tight. Take the loose end and stretch it back to hook into the barb on the hook. Since the rubber band in the spinnerbait eye will be slightly above the hook point, the result will be a hook in which the rubber band completely covers and protects the hook point, while still allowing the rubber band to pop free and hook a fish when one hits.

340

Quick Paint Stirrer

Many of the paints you use on jigs, poppers, and other lures are hard to mix by hard shaking when the bottles are full. And as the paint gets older and thicker, it gets even tougher to mix thoroughly. You could use a stick to stir the paint, but there's a method that's quicker and not as messy.

Drop a buckshot, small bullet (not the whole cartridge), or large split-shot into the bottle. As you shake the bottle, the pellet stirs up the paint.

341

Finding the Leak

A leak in a hollow plastic plug reduces the lure's buoyancy and may ruin its action. If a plug isn't running right, shake it while holding the hooks and split rings against the body so they don't rattle. If you hear water inside, you've found the problem.

Lower the lure, which has been frozen, into hot water. The rapid warming will cause the cold air in the lure to expand and bubble out of the leak, pinpointing its location. Shake out water if you can. If not, suck the water out through the leak or enlarge the hole with a hot pin. Patch the leak with epoxy.

342

Remembering the Right Crankbait

Different crankbaits run at different depths. If you're fishing in 8 feet (2.4 m) of water, you'll probably want a lure that runs 6 or 7 feet (1.8 or 2 m) deep. If you can't recall how deep your crankbaits run, try marking them.

Write the running depth of each lure on the body or lip with an indelible marker so you know at a glance which crankbait to use. Running depths are often listed in catalogs or the instructions that come with the lures, but it's best to test them yourself. Different line weights and retrieve speeds cause the lures to run at different depths.

343

Fixing the Weak Link

You hook a big fish, it thrashes wildly, but then it's gone.

After you reel in, you find a hook is missing from your lure. A split ring broke and the fish swam off with the hook.

This all-too-common problem can be prevented by soldering your split rings to keep them from pulling apart. Even if you have a soldering gun handy, however, you may have trouble getting the solder to stick.

Beef up your split rings so they won't break at a critical moment.

344

Hook Big Fish Better

Most plugs, spoons, and spinners come with treble hooks. But if you're after trophy-class fish, ordinary trebles may not be strong enough. Big-fish specialists know that a good-sized single hook sinks deeper and holds better than a treble and no fish is likely to bend or break it.

If you're fishing in waters where there's a good chance of hooking something big, replace your trebles with single Siwash hooks. A Siwash has a sturdy shank and an extra-long slow-tapering point that penetrates like a needle. Once a fish is on, there's little chance it will get away.

Lures with a single Siwash hook offer another advantage: they can be used in waters where treble hooks are banned.

If the trebles are attached with split rings, you can simply open the ring, take off the treble, and substitute the Siwash. If the ring is welded, you'll have to cut it off and add a new one. If a lure has two or three trebles, you may want to remove all of them and add just one Siwash where the rear treble was. Changing hooks may disrupt the lure's balance and ruin its action, so be sure to test it before fishing.

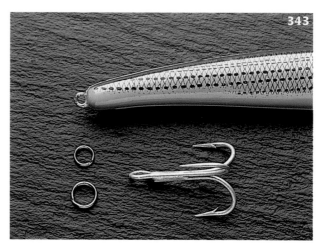

1. Remove the original split ring and treble hook. Find two split rings that nestle together, so one fits snugly inside of the other.

2. Join the hook and plug with the small ring first. Start the large ring on the plug (shown), then put it on the hook. A split-ring pliers makes the job easier.

3. Fit the small ring inside the larger one. Often, it snaps into place. Even if it doesn't fit snugly, the connection has been strengthened.

345

Stick Rattle in Soft Plastics

One way to increase the attractiveness of a saltwater shrimp or minnow bait is to add a rattle in it for noise when it is twitched along the bottom.

346

Add Glow Stick to Lure for Deep Walleye Fishing

Glow sticks are available from many hobby, general, and tackle stores. These are small Cyalume sticks that, when bent, break an internal glass container to mix substances to produce a cold light, similar that of fireflies. These small sticks are generally 1½ or 2 inches (3.8 to 5 cm) long and about ⅛-inch (3 mm) diameter. Attach these small sticks to lures to produce light and attract fish when deep fishing. The best way to attract a light stick is to use clear tape and tape it around the hook shank of jigs or onto the body of deep jigging spoons. They can also be attached with clear tape to the leader or line just above a baited hook.

347

Insert BBs into Crankbait Bodies

It is easy to add rattles, noise, and some weight to a hollow crankbait. To do this, drill a small ³⁄₁₆-inch-hole (4.7 mm) into the belly of the crankbait and insert one or more BBs. Then seal the hole with a dab of five-minute epoxy glue. While doing this, make sure that you hold the lure with the belly up so the BBs do not adhere to the dab of glue sealing the hole.

1. Use a small stick or large nail and insert it into the head or thick area of the shrimp or baitfish to make a hole into which to insert a rattle. Carefully insert the rattle into the hole, pushing it all the way in so it does not come out when fished.

2. If making a lot of rattle lures, another way is to use a length of thin copper or brass tubing such as is available from hobby shops. Tubing from about ¹⁄₁₆ to ⅛ inch (1.6 to 3 mm) works best. Sharpen the edge of one end of the tubing. Core out a hole, then rotate the tubing to break off and remove the plastic core.

3. The hole in the soft plastic makes it easier to insert the rattle and also holds the rattle in place more securely. Remove the core from the tubing with a toothpick, kabob skewer, or length of straight wire coat hanger.

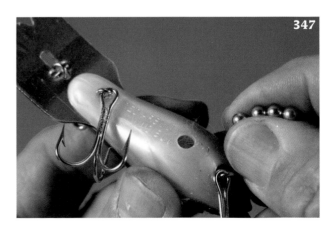

348

High-Vis Dry Flies

Dry flies can be tough to see as it gets dark. And if you can't see a dry fly, it's tough to fish it. You can make dry flies that are visible, even in low light.

349

Pinch-On Sinker Adds Weight to Jig Hook

Use the blade of a screwdriver to open up the slot on a pinch-on sinker so you can add it to a jig or bucktail shank for more weight. This is particularly good when saltwater fishing so you can get deep without going to a jig or bucktail larger than what the fish might want.

350

Tooth-Proof Streamers

Toothy gamefish cut ordinary tinsel-bodied streamers to shreds. Streamer bodies made by slipping woven Mylar tubing over the shank aren't very durable, either. If a few individual strands are cut, the body unravels.

You can use that same Mylar tubing (with the string core removed) to make a much tougher streamer. Because the Mylar is wrapped on, the strands bind one another to the shank, so the fly won't fall apart, even if several are cut.

Tie in a tuft of fluorescent yellow or chartreuse steelhead yarn where the wing would be. Then wind the hackle "parachute" style around the base of the yarn rather than the hook. This method keeps the hackle from hiding the yarn, which will be easy to see, even at dusk. But trout see the fly in silhouette and won't be spooked by the color.

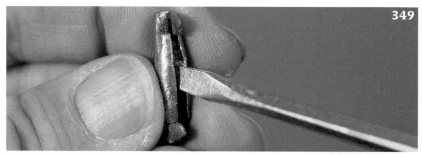

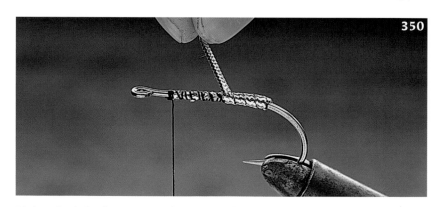

Make a body by first putting a few wraps of thread around the shank. Lay the Mylar along the hook, wrap thread over it, then wrap the Mylar around the shank. Tie off the Mylar with thread. Continue tying the fly.

351

Tune Lure by Shaving Lip

One way to adjust lure movement on lures with plastic lips (most of them) is to shave the side of the lip with a pocket knife. If the lure is running to the right as you face it on retrieve, shave the left side of the lip as you face the lure. If running to the left, shave the right side of the lure. In each case and with each method, try the lure in the water as you do this so you do not overcompensate this correction.

352

Tune Lure by Bending Eye

Lipped crankbaits may or may not run true when right out of the box or may run crooked in time as they are banged around when fishing. One way to correct this is to slightly bend the line tie to position it in the center of the lure. Most line ties are vertical, so you can slightly move the line tie to the right or left. If a lure runs to the right as you look at it coming toward you on retrieve, hold the lure facing you and slightly move the line tie to the left. If the lure runs to the left, move the line tie to the right when holding and facing it.

353

Glue Fishing Knots

Experts tell us that fishing knots only fail when they start to slip. To help prevent this or increase the strength of a knot, use glue. Most tackle shops carry fishing glues, which are waterproof, low-viscosity cyanoacrylate glues similar to the "super glues" sold in hardware stores. Add a little of the glue after pulling the knot tight, since these very thin glues "wick" through the knot to seal and glue it, decreasing the possibility of failure.

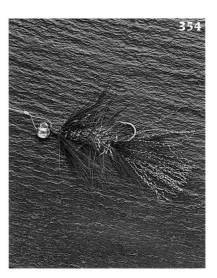

Tie the fly to the tippet with a Duncan loop. Hold the fly with the hook point up, and clamp a split-shot (BB or larger) to the lower strand of the loop. The weight keeps the point riding up so you'll snag less.

354

Snag-Resistant Wooly Buggers

The Wooly Bugger is one of the best flies for big trout and smallmouth bass. Most anglers fish it deep, with a split-shot next to the hook eye, so it moves up and down like a jig. Using a split-shot rather than tying the fly on a jig head allows you to change weight for varying circumstances. But the hook point rides down as often as up and frequently snags on rocks.

355

Weedless Poppers

Most fly rod poppers aren't weedless, so they hang up in the heavy cover where bass hide. Here's how you can make two types of weedguards that allow your popper to slip through weeds and brush.

356

Don't Feed Pelicans When Cleaning Fish

Pelicans often hang around saltwater fish cleaning stations and are always begging for scraps, fillet skeletons and offal. They also hang around fishing piers, jetties and surf areas begging for small bait fish caught and discarded. Do not feed these or other species of birds that are begging for food. First, it is may be illegal in some areas. Second, it does the birds a disservice by not allowing them to forage on their own. Third, too many fillet skeletons or too large a food fish can cause the bones to puncture the stomach wall of birds, causing a slow and agonizing death. Don't do it.

357

Add Tail Hook to Worm

Sometimes fish strike short and thus miss the hook buried Texas-style in the head of a plastic worm. To prevent this, add a hook to the rear of the worm. The best worms for this rigging are those that have some bulk in the tail so you have something into which to bury the hook. First, tie the hook to the line and then thread the hook through the head of the worm and back out of the body, just as if you were making a standard Texas worm rig. Then thread the worm and line through the worm one or two more times until reaching the tail. Do the same thing here, but then make sure the shank of the hook stays buried in the worm and the hook point is rotated to be buried in the worm to make the rig weedless.

1. Mono weedguard. Poke a pair of holes on each side of the hook shank using a needle. Angle the holes out and back. Dip the ends of a piece of 30-pound-test (13.6 kg) mono in 5-minute epoxy and insert them into the holes to form a loop just large enough to protect the hook.

2. Wire weedguard. Punch a needle (1) through the lip of the popper on either side of the hook eye to make a pair of holes. Bend a short length of stainless steel wire (about 0.010-inch [0.3 mm] diameter) so it has a tight loop in the middle. (2) Push the legs of the wire down the holes. (3) Fit the loop over the hook eye, then pull the wire legs to tighten the loop. Trim the legs so they are just long enough to protect the hook point.

Enlightened Fishing

As the sun sinks below the horizon, a red-hot evening bite suddenly turns ice-cold. What happened? Is it possible the fish simply couldn't find your lure in the dark?

That may indeed be the case. When the sun goes down, light penetration may be reduced to the point where fish cannot see your bait. Lack of sufficient light is obviously a problem early or late in the day, but it may also be a problem in midday if it is overcast or windy; if the lake is covered by ice and snow; or if the water is deep or murky.

One way you can beat the low-light problem is to doctor your lures with luminescent tape or paint. The tape can be applied when you're fishing and is much easier to work with than paint. Be sure to use tape that is thin and flexible so it molds to the shape of your lure.

Use flexible luminescent tape for easy application. Don't cover the whole lure with tape. A small spot or strip is enough to attract a fish's attention.

359

Add Rattle to Jig with Rubber Tubing

Slide a piece of rubber tubing over the point and bend of a jig to position the tubing on the shank where you can add a rattle for more noise in your lure. Straight rattles in glass, plastic, and metal are available for this.

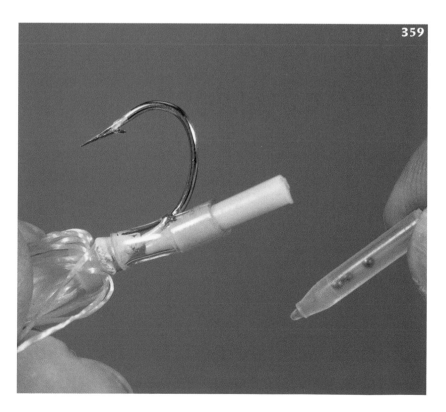

Tips and tricks are not limited to lures and baits. There are helpful ideas for modifying rods and reels, making special tackle accessories for easier fishing and better success, along with dealing with rod, reel, and tackle accessory repairs.

Here are some of the best of tips for all types of fishing. Check them out and see what works for you.

360

Deodorizing Flies

Some flies are tied with materials that have had chemical treatments during manufacture or have been stored with moth balls. To deodorize flies before using them, rub them carefully in mud, seaweed, underwater grasses, or similar natural materials. Wash off these materials, check the fly for proper appearance, and then tie it on and fish.

361

Use Grub, Worm Tails for Fake Leeches

Out of leeches for your walleye fishing? Out of artificial soft plastic leeches? A good substitute is to use the end of a damaged black worm with a flat or flap tail. Cut off the tail, if possible round off the cut end with a flame (cigarette lighter), and then attach it to a hook just as you would any live or artificial leech. To avoid sacrificing good worms for this, save all damaged worms for possible use.

362

Tame Springy Mono

When first put on a spinning reel, heavy mono may spring from the spool as you open the bail, making casting difficult. You have the opposite problem with old line: it's so coiled it doesn't peel off the reel and pass through the guides smoothly.

363

Don't Cross Their Eyes

It's widely believed that the best way to set the hook is to jerk the rod as hard as you can and "cross their eyes." A solid hook set catches more fish, but there's a better way to sink the hooks than jerking wildly, especially if you're using mono line.

If you have any slack in your line, a fast jerk of the rod exerts practically no force at the end of the line. If you find this hard to believe, try the following experiment. Tie a swivel to your line and have someone squeeze it between his or her fingers. With the rod in your hand, back off about 50 feet (15 m). Let out a little extra line and then jerk as hard as you can. Chances are you won't pull the swivel from your partner's fingers. Because of the slack and the stretch of monofilament, surprisingly little force is transmitted.

Here's a better way to get a powerful hook set. When you feel a bite, point your rod at the fish and immediately reel up slack until you feel weight. Then set the hook with a quick snap of the wrists.

Although this hook-setting method is much less spectacular, it transmits considerably more force for driving in the hooks.

364

Better Grip for Grubs

A plastic grub used to tip a spinnerbait or buzzbait tends to slide down the hook and lose action. The skirt covers the hook collar, so the grub rides on the shank, where there's nothing to hold it. Solve the problem by putting a drop of super glue on the shank before sliding the grub into place.

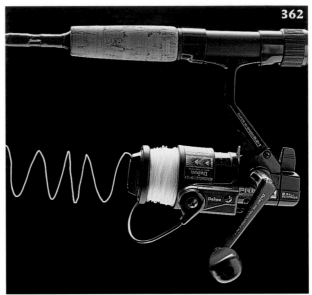

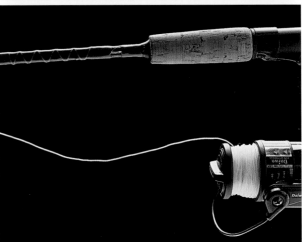

Coiled mono or line that springs off the reel can be softened by soaking your spool in warm tap water for about 10 minutes. When you put the spool back on the reel, the line will be much more manageable.

365

Budget Line Stripper

Removing old line by hand is tedious. You can buy a line stripper to make the job easier. But either way, you end up with a tangled pile of line you can't reuse.

If you're stripping off expensive line, such as braided Dacron or lead-core, you'll probably want to save it. This makes the job even more time-consuming because you have to wind the line onto another spool.

To remove line quickly and save it to use another time, put a 6- to 8-inch (15 to 20 cm) dowel in the chuck of an electric drill. Tie the line to the dowel and run the drill at low to medium speed until all the line is removed. With a baitcasting reel, use the clicker or your thumb to keep the spool from overrunning and causing a backlash.

When the line is on the dowel, secure it as shown in the photo.

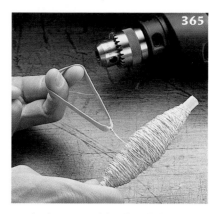

Tie the line to a rubber band, then put the rubber band around the dowel so the line doesn't unravel.

366

Breaking in Buzzbaits

Many bass anglers find that one buzzbait catches more than all their others—even those that seem identical. Chances are, the bait that works so well is old and beat up. The wear and tear on the prop pivot holes cause it to make more noise than a new lure and that noise attracts bass. Here's a simple way to break in your new buzzbaits so they make as much noise and catch as many fish as the old ones do: Remove the prop and drive the tip of a square masonry nail into the pivot holes to make them square. Reassemble the lure. The larger, square holes make the blade rattle on the shaft.

1. Split-shot dropper. Tie the leader to a barrel swivel. Tie the line to the other eye, leaving a tag end several inches (cm) long for a couple of split-shot. This rig uses one less knot than a three-way swivel rig, yet it works the same way: if the sinkers hang up, a hard tug pulls them off the dropper, as you get the rest of your rig back.

367

Easy Pull-Off Sinker Rigs

If you're fishing a bait rig over a rocky bottom, it's a good idea to use a sinker that will pull off if the weight hangs up in rocks. That way, you just add a new sinker rather than make a whole new rig. But tying most pull-off sinker rigs takes time. The line, leader, and dropper are usually attached to a three-way swivel, requiring three knots. Two simpler rigs that take less time to make are shown in the photos.

2. Pencil-lead dropper. Slide a 1-inch (2.5 cm) piece of surgical tubing over your line. Jam the lead about ¼ inch (6 mm) into the tubing. Slide the tubing to the desired distance above your hook. If the lead snags bottom, a hard tug will pull it out of the sleeve. If it pulls out too easily, increase the friction by pushing it farther into the tubing.

368

The Cat's-Paw Connection

Double-strand leaders save lots of fish, but the way most anglers tie them, the hook will pull off if one strand breaks. Solve the problem with a "cat's-paw," a knot used by many saltwater anglers to attach a hook to a double-strand leader. The knot holds the hook securely, even if a fish bites through one strand.

369

Conserve Rubber Stops

The small rubber stops you buy already threaded on a wire loop make handy sinker or bobber stops. Simply slip them from the wire loop onto the line and slide them into position. The rubber won't scuff your line the way other stops sometimes do.

But the stops are fairly expensive and once you take them off the line, they're difficult to put back on because the hole is too small to push the line through. You could rethread them with a sewing needle, but there's an easier way.

370

Handy J-Plug Box

J-Plugs and similar conical trolling plugs with removable hook harnesses are popular for salmon and many anglers carry dozens of them. To prevent tangling, some fishermen store the hooks and plug bodies separately. But the bodies take up a lot of space in a tackle box and if you file them together in the same tray, you risk damaging the finish. Protect the plugs' finish and keep them in order, making it easy to find the one you want.

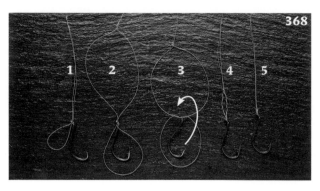

Tie a 1-foot (30 cm) loop in your line with a strong knot, such as a double surgeon's loop, and (1) thread the loop through the hook eye. (2) Spread the loop and the two leader strands, and (3) pass the hook through the loop and between the two leader strands (arrow) about five times. (4) Start to tighten the knot by holding the hook while pulling with the standing line. (5) Moisten the knot, then pull it snug. The finished knot resembles the pads of a cat's paw.

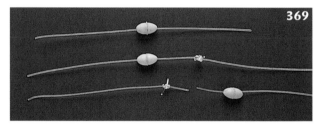

Save a rubber stop by cutting it off along with a section of your old mono. To reuse the stop, tie the piece of old mono to your new line. Push the stop over the knot onto the new line, then cut off the knot. Slide the stop into the desired position.

Modify a tackle box by cutting a sheet of plastic, plywood, or durable packing foam so it fits snugly in the box as shown. Drill rows of holes large enough to accommodate the plug bodies. Put the holder in place and set the plugs in the holes, head up. Store the hook harnesses in a separate container.

371

Quick and Easy Line Holder

It's a good idea to carry extra spools of line. But spools lying loose in a tackle box take up a lot of space and are almost sure to tangle with your tackle. Here's an easy-to-build rack that keeps line in order and fits in a storage compartment in your boat.

Nail or screw together a three-sided rack from scrap lumber. Drill a ⅜-inch (1 cm) hole completely through one end piece and partly through the other. Slide a ⅜-inch dowel through the first hole and seat it in the opposite hole. Trim the dowel flush with the outside of the end piece.

Nail or screw a small metal flap to the end piece to cover the end of the dowel and keep it from sliding out. The flap pivots so you can remove the dowel.

Put a rubber band around each spool to keep the line from unwinding. Slide the dowel through the spools, seat it and drop the flap. Keep a nail clipper handy by tying it to the rack with a short piece of fishing line.

372

Save Your Slip Bobber

When slip-bobber fishing, your sinker may snag and you'll have to break the line. Without the sinker to stop it, the bobber slides off and you have to chase it.

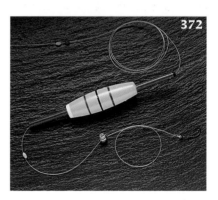

Tie a slip-bobber rig as you normally would, with a bobber stop above the float. Then add a second bobber stop below the float; it should ride just above the sinker. Now if you break off the sinker, the extra stop keeps the bobber from sliding off.

373

Use Dropper and Downrigger to Get Light Lures Deep

Cut your fishing line several feet (m) from the end and then retie with a blood knot, leaving a long tag end from the main line. Then tie your lure to the end of your retied line (not the dropper) for fishing. This allows you to use the tag end dropper in the clip of a downrigger outfit so you can fish deep with light tackle. It will not hurt the fishing outfit if the tag end of dropper gets frayed from being pulled repeatedly from the downrigger clip as fish hit. This is an ideal way to fish very light tackle with typical downrigger fishing rigs.

374

Vest-Pocket Tackle Box

Anglers who wade or hike in to fishing spots have to keep their gear compact as well as orderly. Organize small items such as leaders, hooks, and spinner blades when space is limited.

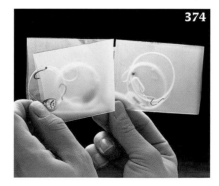

Slip coiled leaders and other small, flat items into the sleeves of a credit card wallet.

375

Bobber Getter

Large cylindrical slip-bobbers are popular with shore-bound catfish anglers. The floats are quite expensive, so it's painful to break your line on a snag and watch your float drift slowly from sight. Some ingenious anglers recover their floats.

376

Straighten up Snaps and Swivels

The right snap, swivel, or hook is hard to find if you dump all your terminal tackle into one or two compartments of your tackle box. You can find these small items more easily if you sort them by size and string them on safety pins or paper clips.

377

A Clip-Slip Bobber

If you need a slip-bobber but have only a common round clip bobber (everybody has at least one), try the simple trick shown in the photo.

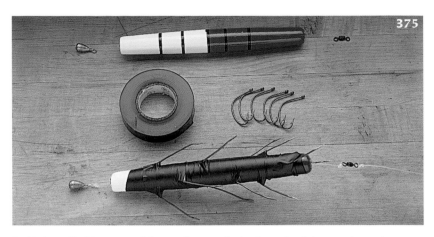

1. Make a "bobber getter" from a large cylinder float. Straighten a dozen large hooks, clip off the eyes, and shove the shanks into the float so the points angle toward one end. Wrap electrical tape around the float and the base of the spines to reinforce them. Run heavy mono through the float. Tie a barrel swivel to the end the hooks point toward and a ⅜-ounce (11 g) sinker to the other end. The sinker provides casting weight and tips the float but won't sink it.

2. Cast the bobber getter beyond the free-floating bobber. Retrieve it to within a few inches (cm) of the drifting float. Then jerk the rod to sink the spines.

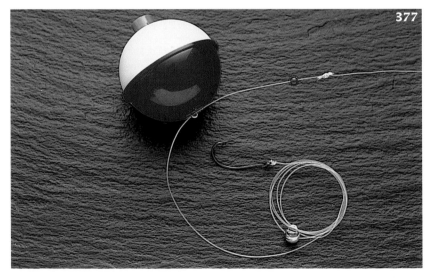

Depress the button, pushing out the bottom clip. Turn the button to rotate the clip 180 degrees so it rests on the bobber rather than seating in the hole. Thread a bobber stop onto your line, add the hook and sinker, then clip on the bobber.

378

Better Spring-Lock Bobber

Many anglers like spring-lock bobbers because the long upper tip telegraphs light bites and is easy to see. But these floats have a couple of drawbacks: They are held on the line by a metal spring that may kink and weaken the monofilament. Also, pulling hard on a fish or snag can lift the spring, causing the bobber to pop off the line.

You need to modify the float to solve these problems.

379

Ultralong Ultralights

Short ultralight spinning rods are ideal for fishing in tight, brushy cover. But longer ultralights are a better choice for most other circumstances. They have extra flex for casting light lures, cushion light line against the thrashing of a fish, and give you better line control and stronger hook sets. Unfortunately, long ultralight rods are hard to find.

Build your own from a 3- to 5-weight graphite fly rod blank. Outfit the rod with the handle, reel seat, and guides you would put on a standard spinning rod.

380

Use Saliva on Knots

According to the experts, saliva has enzymes that can hide or disguise other scents that might repel fish. In addition, fish are not repelled by the smell of saliva. Thus, spitting on your bait or lure and using saliva as a lubricant when pulling up knots can't hurt and might possibly help in catching more fish. In addition, as a lubricant, you know that you have tight, secure fishing knots.

381

Keep Skirts Pliable

The rubbery skirts on spinnerbaits, jigs, and Hula Poppers tangle and get stiff as they age, losing their appealing action. There's a way to keep them pliable.

Replace the spring with a ½-inch (13 mm) piece of surgical rubber tubing that fits snugly over the lower stem. Thread the line through the tubing, then push it into the notch in the stem. Slide the tubing up over the notch. Roll back the tubing to move the bobber. The soft rubber does not kink the line and even the strongest pull won't cause the bobber to pop off.

Spray the skirts with Armor All protectant, sold in auto stores to keep vinyl upholstery in good condition. Wipe off the excess with a cloth.

382

Getting Pigs off Jigs

New pork chunks can be hard to get off hooks because the hole is too small to pass over the barb. Try this method to get the pig off your jig: twist the pork chunk hard one way and then the other to enlarge the hole. Then stretch the hole over the barb and slide the pork off the hook.

383

Organize Your Worm Hooks

Rummaging through loose worm hooks is a hassle. If your hooks aren't sorted by size and type, you can run short of the ones you need without knowing it.

Bind the hooks of each type and size together with a rubber band. You'll be able to find the proper bundle and slip a hook out in a moment.

384

Fixing Sticky Ferrules

The graphite ferrules on some fishing rods often stick together. Pulling them apart is a hassle and if you're not careful you may damage or break the rod. If you have a ferrule that sticks, try rubbing the male section with ordinary pencil lead. The thin film of graphite lubricates the connection. After your next fishing trip, the rod should pull apart easily.

385

No-Slip Crimps

To attach a swivel or other terminal tackle to braided wire line or downrigger cable, you can make a loop in the wire and crimp a metal sleeve over the wire and tag end. But if the crimp loosens, you lose tackle. Crimp the wire so it won't pull out.

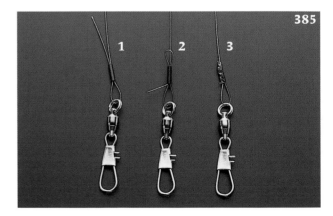

Thread the wire (1) through the sleeve, through the swivel eye, and back through the sleeve. (2) Push the tag end of the wire back through the sleeve. Pull the end to snug up the loop, but don't pull the loop into the sleeve. (3) Crimp the sleeve with a crimping tool; clip the tag end.

386

Leader Tamer

Tossed loose in your tackle box, pre-tied rigs such as leaders, worm harnesses, and snelled hooks end up a hopeless mess. Keep them from tangling while removing any kinks.

387

No-Drip Rod Finish

The thin epoxy used on rod wraps is more durable than other finishes but has this fault: it forms drips before it hardens, unless the rod is held in a horizontal position and rotated. Rod builders often use small, low-speed motors to do this job. Otherwise, you'll have to rotate the rod a quarter turn every 30 seconds for the first half-hour and less often during the next hour as the epoxy thickens. It's a good job to do while watching television. If you don't have the patience to rotate the rod by hand, try this: Brush on two very thin coats of the glossy polyurethane finish used on wood. Or use a quick-setting rod finish, such as Speed Coat. If applied sparingly, neither of these finishes drip and no turning is necessary.

388

Controlling Leader Coils

Long wire and mono leaders are a nuisance to store. If you coil them and then wrap an end several times around the coils, it can be tough unwrapping the leader when you want to use it. Taping the coil is time-consuming and difficult to undo.

389

Easy-Spinning Spinners

Most spinner-and-bait rigs have a series of beads between the hook and clevis. Sometimes friction between the clevis and the last bead prevents the blade from turning freely, especially on a slow retrieve. A simple modification that lets the blade spin more easily is shown in the photo.

Stretch out your pre-tied leaders after sinking the hooks in the edge of a piece of durable packing foam. Pin the loop of each leader to the foam, using an ordinary hook as a staple.

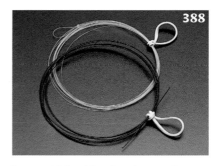

Loop a thick rubber band around one side of the coil and cinch it up tight. No knot is necessary, so you can unwrap the leader in a hurry.

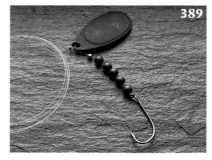

Add a very small bead between the clevis and the larger beads. The small bead has less surface area, reducing friction against the clevis.

Do You Get the Point?

Everyone knows that sharp hooks are important, yet few anglers take time to sharpen their hooks. To make matters worse, they often buy the cheapest hooks rather than spend a little extra to get good sharp ones.

The photos depict just how dull some hooks really are and show the best ways to ensure that your hooks are sharp.

Ordinary hooks (1) are surprisingly dull. You can (2) sharpen them to a triangular point with a file or hook hone. (3) Chemically sharpened hooks are even sharper than filed hooks, but they cost up to 10 times more. (4) A good motorized sharpener makes the keenest point of all, though they're a bit too bulky to carry if you fish on foot. One of the best is the Pointmatic Hook-Hone-R, which is easy to use and has long-lasting rechargeable batteries

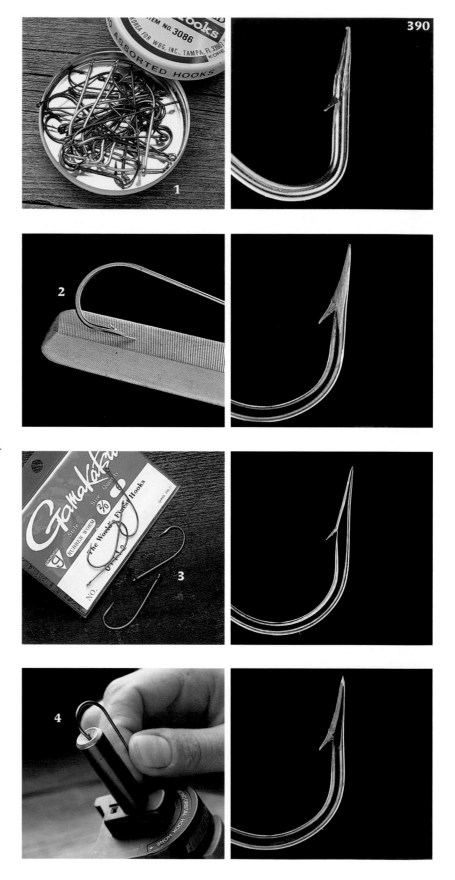

391

Better Hook Sets with Diving Planes

Diving planes work well for deep trolling, but setting the hook may be a problem. Because of the water resistance of the planer, the full force of your hook set doesn't reach the fish.

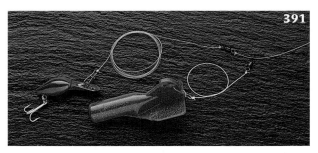

Tie about a foot of heavy monofilament and a barrel swivel to the front clip of a diving plane such as a Luhr Jensen Jet Planer. Run your line through the other end of the swivel and tie it to a second swivel, fastened to a leader and your lure. The diving plane now slides along your line, much as a slip-sinker does. When a fish strikes, it pulls enough line through the swivel so you pull directly against the fish when you set the hook.

392

Waterproofing Maps

Lake and river maps are always near water. If the maps you use while fishing aren't water-resistant, protect them this way. Apply a waterproof sealant such as Thompson's Water Seal, designed for treating concrete block and wood. Spread the sealant on both sides of the map with a foam varnish brush. Cover the surface, but don't drench it. Use clothespins to hang the map from a line until it dries.

393

Coil Fly Lines in Large Loops For Storage

To prevent tight coils in your fly line and the resultant difficulties in casting, store your lines during the off season by removing them from reels and hanging them in large loose loops. To keep these from tangling during the off season, fasten each coil with several pipe cleaners, twisting the pipe cleaner around the line at three different spots on each coil.

394

Cane Pole Line Holder

Two-piece cane poles and telescoping poles are usually rigged with a line about as long as the pole. When you collapse or un-joint the pole, you have extra line and nowhere to put it. Here's a solution.

Tape two paper clips to the rod near the butt. Space them about 3 feet (0.9 m) apart with their opposite ends exposed. After you break down the rod, wrap the extra line between the clips.

395

Bundle Rods Quickly

When storing or transporting two-piece rods without a case, it's a good idea to bundle the easily damaged tip with the stiffer butt section. But putting rubber bands where you want them and getting them off again can be difficult. The photo shows a simple way to put a rubber band whenever there's a guide.

396

Easy Hook Keeper

A hook keeper near the rod butt comes in handy, yet many rods don't have one. Make a hook keeper from materials you have on hand.

397

Prevent Fly Rod Hang-Ups

When a big salmon, trout, or saltwater fish grabs your fly and makes a run, any knot or tangle in the fly line can hang up in the guides, popping one off or snapping the tippet. If you build your own rods, you can reduce the chances of this happening.

Use stripper guides, snake guides, and a tiptop that are all a bit larger than you'd find on a commercially made rod built on the same blank. A knot in the line stands a better chance of clearing these larger guides without damage to the rod or tippet.

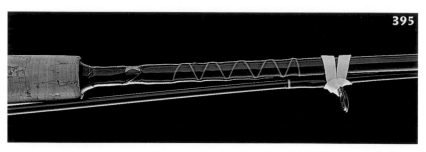

Loop a rubberband around a guide. Wrap it around rod sections once or twice, and loop over guide again.

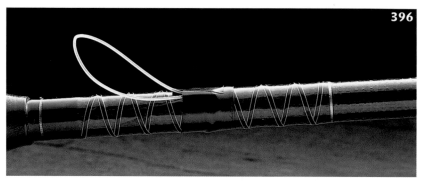

1. Tape down the ends of a loop made from 5 inches (13 cm) of heavy mono. The loop should point toward the rod butt.

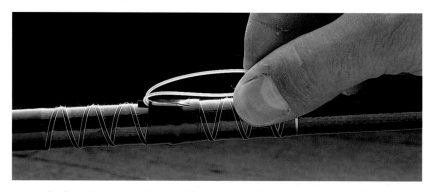

2. Lay the loop back over the tape. The loop should now point toward the rod tip.

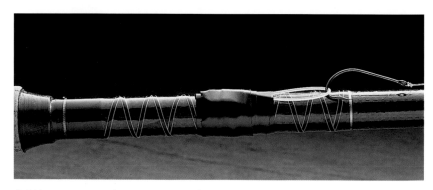

3. Wrap tape over the mono two or three more times. Slip the hook into the loop.

398

Long-Distance Baitcasting

Modern baitcasting reels are precision instruments, capable of casting long distances. But there are times when even longer casts are needed.

Shore fishermen, for instance, may have to make superlong casts to reach fish in mid-river or to reach a drop-off in a lake.

If distance is important, you can modify an ordinary baitcasting reel to reduce friction against the spool, allowing you to cast a heavy lure or sinker 100 yards (91.4 m) or even farther. Because the spool will spin much more freely, you'll have to thumb the reel more skillfully to avoid backlashes. You can get extra distance from your reel.

399

Keep Cold Metal Under Wraps

One of the coldest things about fishing in chilly weather is the metal reel seat of a spinning rod. Keep the cold metal off your hands.

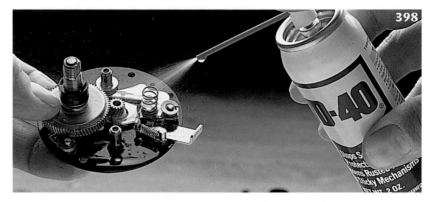

1. Clean out the heavy grease in bearings, gears, the levelwind mechanism, and other moving parts by spraying them with a light lubricant, which dissolves the grease and washes it away.

2. Remove the sleeves that rub against the spool and act as centrifugal brakes. If backlashes are a problem after removing the sleeves, replace one of them. On magnetic reels, remove the small magnets.

3. Fill the spool to increase its circumference. That way, the same number of revolutions of the spool produces a longer cast. Small-diameter line also increases distance; use the lightest line practical for the water you're fishing.

Wrap the reel seat with the tape sold in bike stores to cover handlebars. Another option is the cloth self-adhesive tape that is sold in drug stores and resembles an ACE bandage. Either material insulates your hand from the cold and provides a comfortable grip on the reel seat.

400

Budget Marker Buoys

If you're moving from spot to spot or following a long breakline, it pays to carry a lot of marker buoys. You can make cheap buoys that are as good as the ones you can buy.

401

Airline Emergency Kit

You've shelled out a lot of money for an exotic fishing trip, but when you step off the airplane, your tackle is nowhere to be found. The stores available in many remote locations can't outfit you properly, so your vacation dreams are put on hold until the airline tracks down your fishing gear. In some cases, your tackle never arrives and your fishing trip is ruined. Granted, the chances of losing your tackle in transit are small, but the result is often disastrous. Here's a way to guard against it.

Pack an emergency fishing kit and carry it on the airplane. Pack light because your baggage must fit under the seat or in the overhead luggage compartment. The kit should consist of a rod or two that can be broken down, reels, a spool of line, and a selection of lures and terminal tackle. You may not be able to pack everything you want, but make sure you have enough to get by.

402

No-Tangle Rods

When you carry a bundle of strung-up rods in your boat or car, you invariably end up with a tangle of lines and rod tips. Then, as you go to use a rod, you have to spend time unwrapping it from the other lines before you can fish.

Next time you carry a bunch of rods, try rigging them before tossing them in your rod box or vehicle.

Cut an H-shaped piece from a thick sheet of tough packing foam. Tie one end of a 50-foot (15 m) cord to the center of the H, then wind it on. Attach a 4- to 8-ounce (0.1 to 0.2 kg) sinker to the end of the cord. When you toss out the marker, the cord unwinds as the weight sinks. The marker's flattened shape keeps it form unwinding once the weight hits bottom. If the marker doesn't unwind, use a heavier sinker or cut down the height of the H.

Secure the hook on the reel, grab the line halfway up the rod, wrap it once or twice around the rod, and loop it over a guide. This way the line can't tangle.

403

Case Your Rod and Reel

A long fishing rod is a nuisance when you drive from one fishing spot to another. You can take off the reel and case the rod, which is time-consuming. Or you can break the rod down and, leaving it strung up, toss it in the back seat or trunk, where it's likely to get broken. You can safely stow a spinning, baitcasting, or fly rod in a vehicle without having to unstring it and take off the reel.

404

Ice-Resistant Tiptop

Frozen tiptops plague ice fishermen. The ice clings to the guide struts, sharp metal edges, and ceramic inserts and is hard to remove. Here's how to get rid of the ice easily.

405

Freeing Jammed Ferrules

Graphite ferrules sometimes jam so tight that all the standard ways of freeing them, such as holding the rod behind your knees and pushing out with your legs to separate the joint, don't work. Trying to muscle the sections apart may break the rod. You can get them apart without forcing them.

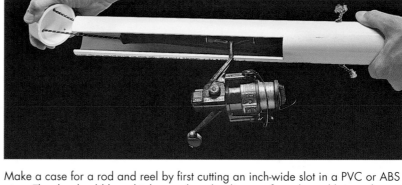

Make a case for a rod and reel by first cutting an inch-wide slot in a PVC or ABS pipe. The slot should be a bit longer than the distance from the rod butt to the reel seat. Drill a hole in each side of the pipe, about a foot from the end, and two more holes in a cap that fits the pipe. Thread elastic shock cord through the hole and knot the ends. The cord keeps the cap on snugly, but you can pull it off to put a rod in the tube. Glue a permanent cap on the other end.

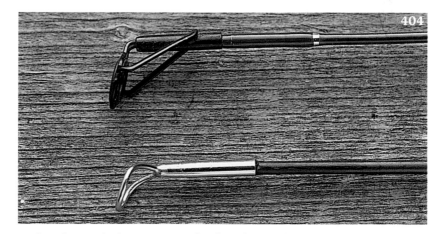

Replace the standard tiptop (top) with a fly rod tiptop (bottom). It has a much smoother shape, no struts, and the thin wire has less surface area to collect ice. Any ice that forms is easily removed with your fingers.

1. Cool the ferrule by placing ice cubes on it or simply leaving the rod outside in cool weather. Both sections of the ferrule contract.

2. Grasp the female ferrule at the end. Hold it for 20 seconds; it warms and expands before the male section does, so you can easily separate the two.

406

Wear-Resistant Tiptop

Winter lake-trout anglers often use braided wire line for vertical jigging in very deep water. Wire line stretches less than mono or Dacron, making it much easier to detect strikes. But wire cuts through tiptops like a hacksaw. You could use a tiptop with a line roller, but it may ice up in cold weather. Make a tiptop that will stand up to wire line and won't freeze up.

407

Use Split Shot to Adjust Carolina Rig

One easy way to make an adjustable Carolina rig is to use a split shot on the line to hold the egg sinker in place. Use this in place of a tied-on swivel. The split shot allows moving the shot up and down on the line so you can adjust the position of the egg sinker in relation to the worm on the end of the line.

408

Cork Caulk

If your dog chews up the cork handle of your best fishing rod or a toothy fish takes a chunk out of a popper, don't worry. Here's an easy way to repair gouges in cork.

Fill the gouges with a paste made by mixing 5-minute epoxy and cork sawdust. Sand the filler flush with the cork after it hardens. Rod builders create a lifetime supply of cork sawdust when they turn down rod handles. Otherwise, get the sawdust you need by filing on a large cork.

1. Fill a brass tube 6 inches (15 cm) long and ³⁄₁₆ inch (5 mm) in diameter with sand. Tape the ends closed to keep the sand from spilling out of the tube.

2. Bend the tube in a right angle around a 1-inch (2.5 cm) dowel or pipe. The sand keeps the tube from collapsing. Pour out the sand; smooth any rough edges.

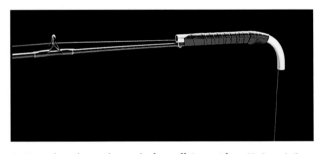

3. Tape the tube to the end of a stiff 3- to 4-foot (0.9 to 1.2 m) rod after removing the old tiptop. The tube lasts because it distributes wear over a large area.

409

No-Slip Tiptop

Anglers commonly replace the broken or damaged tiptops on their rods by bonding them on with ferrule cement. They melt the cement, smear some on the rod, and put on the tiptop. But the tiptop strips off most of the cement as you push it on, so it soon comes loose. Here's how to install a tiptop that won't slip off or twist around on the rod.

Heat the old tiptop to melt the ferrule cement and pull it off with a pliers. Apply cement to the last ¼ inch (6 mm) of the rod and install the new tiptop.

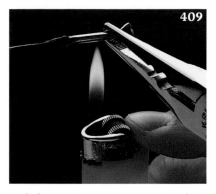

Push the new tiptop partway on and then heat it to draw the cement inside. Push the tiptop on the rest of the way and turn it so it aligns with the other guides.

410

Bank Fisherman's Strike Indicator

When you're bank fishing with your rod propped on stick, a strong wind can buffet the tip. Other times, poor light can make it tough to see the rod tip move. Either way, a bite is hard to detect. You can tell when a fish is biting under these conditions by making a strike indicator.

One way is to clip the eye of a snap-swivel to a small clip bobber and hang the snap on your line between the first and second guides. The bobber rises as a fish takes the bait.

Trouble is, to reel in a fish, you must pull the bobber off the line and that takes time. Then, if you're not careful, the bobber may fall in the water and you'll lose it. The photo shows a rig that solves those problems.

1. Bend 12 inches (30 cm) of stainless steel wire in half and twist a small loop in one end. Push the wire legs through a large cork as shown. Bend the legs outward and then back inward, so they cross and touch. The cork should be painted or wrapped with reflective or luminescent tape so it's more visible. Tie the cork to a ½-ounce (14 g) sinker.

411

Loop on Drop-Shot Rig Prevents Rod Tangles

Bass anglers often fish a variety of lures on several or more rods carried in a boat. When running between spots, it is easy to hook lures into the crossbar of a reel to prevent tangles. To prevent tangles with worm rigs, catch the worm hook on a reel handle or wrap a few turns of the end of the line around the reel. For drop-shot rigs in which the split shot sinkers are on the end of the line below the hook, tie a loop in the line end to hook onto the rod handle or reel handle when running.

2. Hang the wire legs of the strike indicator on the line between the first and second guides. As a fish takes the bait, the strike indicator rises. When a fish runs, line slides through the wire legs. Jerk the cork off the line when you pick up the rod. The tether and sinker keep it from blowing or drifting away.

412

Swivel Gaff

When you hook a big fish on your gaff and it starts thrashing wildly, it can twist the handle out of your hand. You need to keep a grip on the gaff.

413

Double-Duty Fly Rods

Many anglers who wade streams are faced with a difficult choice as they begin to assemble their tackle: fly fishing or spinning? It's tough to carry and fish two rods, so you have to choose. Or do you?

Resolve the dilemma by using your fly rod for both fly fishing and spinning. A fly rod can easily double as a spinning rod. Its length is useful for drifting bait or small jigs and it flexes enough to cast light lures. You'll be ready for anything, no matter what the fish are biting on.

414

Pre-Tie Lures to Leaders in Winter

To make tying knots easier, pre-tie short lengths of line to all possible lures you might use when in your home and before venturing afield. Use short lengths of line—about 2 feet long (60 cm)—and finish by tying a loop knot in the end of the line. Then tie a similar loop knot in the end of your fishing line so you can interconnect the loops for easy lure changes when out in cold weather. Make sure that one loop is large so you can easily slip the lure through the loop when changing tackle.

415

Strong Line-to-Leader Loops

The same wrapping technique used to repair a fly line lets you make a strong loop in the end of the line for attaching your leader. This kind of connection is more durable than the common needle knot and you won't need a mono connector on your line.

Make a swivel gaff by forming a hook from a sharpened metal rod about 20 inches (51 cm) long and ¼ inch (6 mm) in diameter. Thread the last 2 inches (5 cm) of the straight end. A machine shop can do the job. Cut a 1-inch (2.5 cm) hardwood dowel about 8 inches (20 cm) long for the handle and drill a hole through the middle large enough for the rod to turn easily inside. Thread a nut on the rod, followed by a washer, the handle, another washer, and two nuts. Now when a big fish thrashes, the gaff swivels inside the handle, so the fish can't twist the gaff from your hand.

Tape on the spinning reel when you want to spin fish, mounting the reel in the middle of the grip so it feels like a spinning outfit. If you build rods, you can make a straight cork handle without a reel seat and tape either reel wherever you want. Or you can install sliding rings to hold the reels in place. Outfit these combination rods with larger-than-normal guides so coils of mono can pass through with less resistance as you cast.

416

Tying Multi-Strand Leaders

If you're tired of getting bit off by pike or pickerel, tie up a leader from small-diameter wire, such as 12- or 18-pound (5.4 to 8.1 kg) Sevenstrand. This twisted multi-strand material doesn't kink as easily as solid wire and it's thinner than nylon-coated wire. The problem comes in trying to fasten the leader to your lure, snap, or swivel, because multi-strand wire, unlike solid wire, is too springy to twist with your fingers.

417

Use Neoprene Soft Drink Holders for Casting Reel Storage

Neoprene drink holders for drink cans are ideal for storing and holding standard casting reels. Most fit the casting reel without adjustment. If you have a larger diameter casting reel, cut several slits into the sides of the holder, parallel to the height of the holder. That way, the neoprene holder can stretch and still hold the casting reel. It is also possible to cut a wide slot on one side so the can holder slips over the reel with the reel on the rod. This also helps to protect a reel in a boat.

418

A Better Needle Knot

A needle knot is a popular way to connect a fly line and leader. But it's difficult to tie because you must slide heavy mono up the thin core of the fly line. The method shown below offers two advantages over an ordinary needle knot. First, it lets you slide heavy mono up the fly line core more easily. Second, you don't need a knot to join the line and leader, so the connection passes through the rod guides without a hitch.

1. Run the wire through the thin eye of the lure or snap, leaving a 6-inch (15 cm) tag end, and clamp on a forceps.

2. Spin the forceps around the main strand of the leader 10 to 15 times, keeping the wraps close together. The centrifugal force wraps the leader tightly.

3. Clip the tag end of the twisted wire close to the wraps. Attach a small barrel swivel to the other end of the leader in the same way.

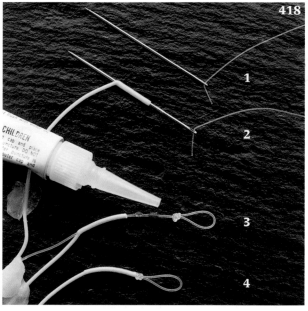

Thread (1) the thin end of a tapered leader through the eye of a needle. (2) Slide the needle up into the fly line core and out the side, about ½ to 1 inch (1.3 to 2.5 cm) from the end. Pull the leader through until the pre-tied loop is within 1 inch (2.5 cm) of the fly line. (3) Coat the leader between the fly line and loop with super glue. (4) Pull the loop snug against the fly line. Trim. Within seconds, the glue bonds the leader securely inside the line, forming a strong splice.

Replacing Rod Guides

Rod guides wear out, they break, they loosen. Or you may just want to replace your guides with better ones. A rod shop could do the job, but so can you.

First, you'll need something to hold the rod while you wrap the guides and apply the finish. You can make a good rod holder from a cardboard box. Cut a straight notch in one side of the box and an L-shaped notch in the other. This way, you can let go of the rod and the weight of the handle won't tip it. When you're done wrapping the rod, the box comes in handy for storing your tools and materials.

Remove the old guides by cutting off the rod windings with a razor blade or X-ACTO knife. Be careful not to nick the rod blank. Remove any hardened epoxy by dampening a cloth with nail polish remover, acetone, or epoxy thinner and holding the rag on the rod for a few moments. Then scrape away the old epoxy with your thumbnail. Now you're ready to put on the new guides.

1. Taper the top of the guide feet with a grinder so the thread wraps on smoothly. If the feet have blunt edges, there will be a gap in the thread at the end of each foot.

2. Run the thread between the pages of a phone book or other heavy book to provide tension as you wrap the guide. The more pages on top of the thread, the greater the tension.

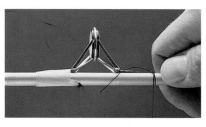

3. Tape down one foot of the guide. Using D-weight nylon winding thread, start wrapping about ¼ inch (6 mm) beyond the tip of the other foot. Turn the rod to wrap the thread over itself.

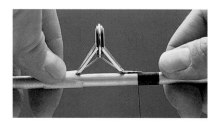

4. Continue to turn the rod, making sure the thread wraps evenly without gaps or overlap. The thread will climb the guide foot smoothly. Trim the tag end of the thread.

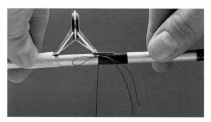

5. Lay down a separate loop of thread when the wraps are about 1⁄16 inch (1.6 mm) from the guide support. Continue wrapping to the support. Clip the thread several inches from the rod.

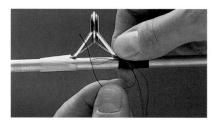

6. Put the tag end of the thread through the loop. As you do this, make sure you hold the last few wraps with your thumb and forefinger so they don't loosen.

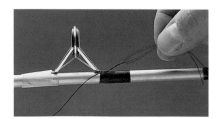

7. Pull the loop to draw the tag end underneath the wraps and out the side. Trim the excess thread. Wrap the other guide foot. Sight down the rod and align the guide.

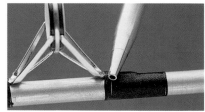

8. Remove any gaps or overlap by gently rubbing across the thread with a smooth, blunt object, such as the barrel of a ballpoint pen.

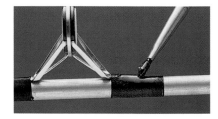

9. Apply rod-winding finish with a brush while turning the rod. Wait a day, trim rough spots with a razor, then add another coat.

420

Stringing up a Fly Rod the Right Way

You rush to get on a trout stream during a big hatch. You're anxious. Time is slipping away. While stringing up your rod, you drop the fly line, which slips backwards through all the guides and lies in a coil near the reel. Now you have to do the job over again.

421

Phosphorescent Tape, Paint for Night Fishing Tackle

Night fishing can be excellent both in freshwater and saltwater. The main disadvantage is that you have to be prepared with your tackle and know where it is at all times. To aid in this, use phosphorescent tape or paint to mark rods, reels, tackle boxes, pliers, gaffs, and other gear you might use and otherwise forget or lose. Some anglers also mark the tip end of their night fishing rods with phosphorescence so they can see the rod tip move when a fish nibbles or hits. This is particularly important if you are using a rod holder and not gripping the rod all the time.

422

Stripping Off Fly Line Coating

Some fly line knots and splices require you to strip several inches of vinyl coating off the line. You could use a wire stripper for the job, but it can nick and weaken the braided core. Or you could use nail polish remover to soften the coating, then strip it off with your thumbnail, but that's messy and inconvenient. The photos show how to avoid these problems.

423

Add Weight to Worm Hook

To keep a worm from spinning when Texas-rigged, use a pinch-on sinker or a few split shot on the hook to act as a keel. To do this, first open the slot in the sinker with a regular screwdriver blade or pocket knife. Slip the hook shank into the sinker slot and then close the sinker with pliers. Note that you can only do this after the hook is placed into the worm in a Texas rig, since the hook shank must travel through the worm body and exit before being buried again in the worm.

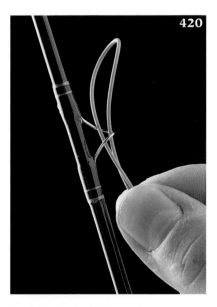

Double over the fly line or butt section of the leader and push the loop through each guide. Now, if you drop the line, the loop springs open and catches in the guide, so you won't have to start over.

Cinch a loop (inset) of 20-pound (9 kg) monofilament onto the fly line, 2 to 3 inches (5 to 7.6 cm) from the end. With the doubled-up mono in one hand and the fly line in the other, pull hard and steady. The mono will cut into the coating and strip it off the core without damaging the core itself. If you have to remove a lot of the coating, strip it off 2 to 3 inches (5 to 7.6 cm) at a time

424

Manageable Marabou

Fluffy marabou streamers and jigs look great in the water. But in the tackle box, the marabou mats down and picks up rust stains from other hooks.

Cut sections of plastic drinking straws a bit longer than the flies or jigs. Cut a slot for the hook in each and slip the tubes over the flies.

425

Repair Damaged Fly Line

The vinyl coating on a fly line is surprisingly tough, but fly lines still get damaged. If a little of the coating gets scraped off, an otherwise perfect line is ruined. The damaged area isn't as stiff as the rest of the line is, so it "hinges" and causes troublesome tangles. The edges of the damaged vinyl hang up in the guides, cutting your casts short. The exposed braided core is subject to abrasion that may weaken the line.

The coating is often damaged when it gets pinched between two metal surfaces, such as the seat and hull of an aluminum boat. If you do damage the line, you will want to repair it, saving an expensive line that still has plenty of life.

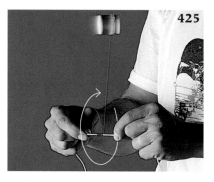

1. Wrap the damaged area with nylon thread or floss by twirling the spool around the line while holding the end of the thread under your thumb. A rubber band around the spool keeps the thread from unwinding.

426

Use Rubber Band on Outrigger for Clip Offshore Trolling

To keep from possibly harming line with an outrigger clip when offshore trolling, loop a rubber band around the line and then fasten the rubber band into the outrigger clip. The rubber band stretches, but pulls out of the clip when a fish hits. If the rubber band does not break, the mate on the boat can pull it free when the rubber band reaches the boat as you play the fish.

2. Guide the thread with your fingertips to cover the damaged area and about ⅛ inch (3 mm) on either side. Perfect wraps aren't needed. Finish the wraps using a loop of thread, just as in wrapping a rod guide.

427

Coil Fly Line in Bucket for Saltwater Boat Casting

When fishing from a boat where you have to be prepared for casting at an instant, use a 5-gallon (22.75 liters) bucket to hold stripped-out fly line. To do this, first strip out a lot of line from the reel, make a cast, and then strip the line into the bucket. The reason is that if you strip line into the bucket before making the cast, the line goes into the bucket in reverse order as it comes out, making tangles a real possibility. With the line in the bucket, you can also store the rod there, ready to be picked up and instantly cast.

3. Coat the thread with a pliable waterproof adhesive, such as Pliobond or GOOP. When the adhesive dries, the repaired area won't hinge and will shoot through the rod guides smoothly.

428

Use Sock on Reel to Protect It

Reels can take a beating in a boat, particularly when banging around on the deck when running to check different spots. To prevent this, carry a few old socks and slip one over each rod/reel combination for reel protection. The sock slightly cushions the reel from damage and also protects it from grime and sand in the boat. For best results, cut a small hole in the sock to fit over the handle end of casting and spinning reels. Do not modify the sock if slipping it over fly reels, which are on the end of the rod. The exception would be those fly outfits with an extension butt. Another possibility with spinning reels is to slip the sock only over the spinning reel, to cover the spool end, housing, and handle and not cover the butt of the rod.

429

Prevent Ice Buildup on Guides

Water on guides and lines can freeze in the winter and make both casting and fishing very difficult. To prevent this, rub a light coating of petroleum jelly onto the guide rings to prevent water and ice build up and to keep lines from sticking. When finished winter fishing, remove the petroleum jelly since during the summer this also picks up dust and grime, which wear lines. This is particularly important when fly fishing.

430

Cover Reel Seats for Winter Fishing Comfort

Cover metal reel seats and parts on the rod with tape when winter fishing to make handling tackle more comfortable. You can use any type of tape, with electricians tape, masking tape, and painters tape high on the list. The best of these is painters tape, which can be easily removed later. With any tape, remove the tape when you are through fishing so the tape does not permanently stick to the tackle.

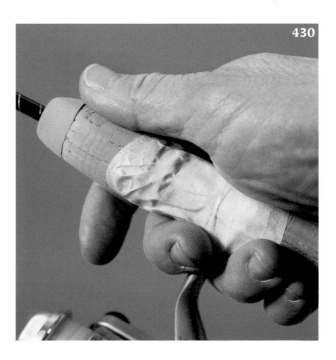

Chapter 5
EQUIPMENT TIPS

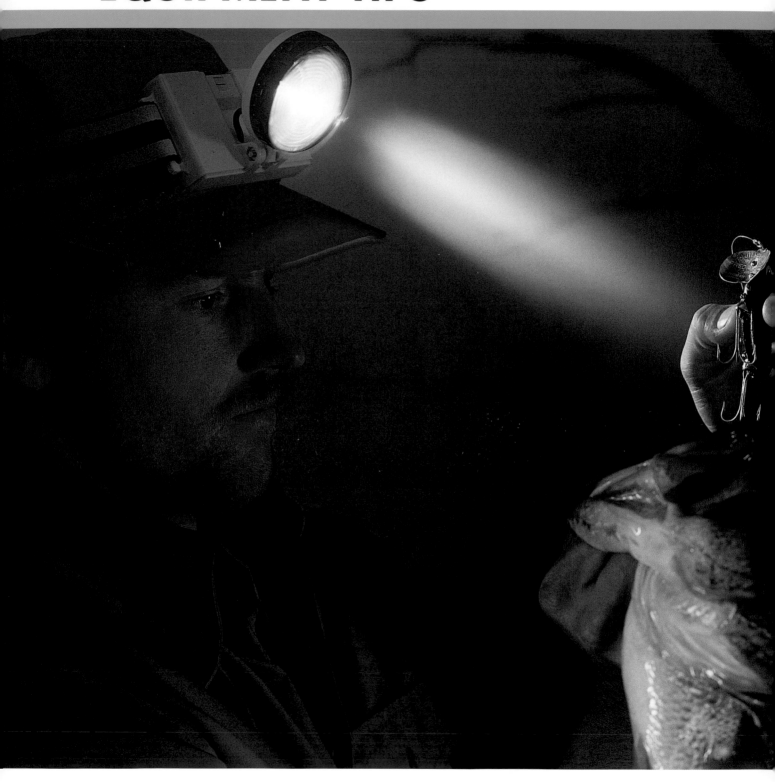

Taking water temperature easily, using old socks to hold spinning spools and protect reels, and cleaning up tackle after a rough trip are all necessary to keep on fishing and having fun.

Keeping your equipment in good order means keeping the fun in fishing. This chapter deals with equipment—how to keep it going and make it better, or fix it quickly and surely when you need to.

431

Use Cord to Remove Hook from Skin

You can use heavy fishing line, fly line, a shoe lace, jacket drawstring, or similar cord to remove hooks. First, remove all other hooks if the caught hook is a lure or use pliers to remove split rings from the hook eye to separate it from the rest of the lure. Loop the cord around the bend of the hook. Use one hand to press down on the shank of the hook and on a quick count, jerk on the cord to pull the hook free. DO NOT do this if the hook is in the face, back of hand, or anywhere there are surface visible veins, arteries, nerves, or tendons. Make sure the victim uses antiseptic on the puncture wound as soon as possible and also checks on tetanus inoculation.

432

Use Reflective Foil on Gas Cans, Coolers

Reflective foil used commercially for covering air conditioners and other outdoor insulation uses is also ideal for covering fishing and boating equipment such as gas cans, coolers, lunch containers, and such. The reflective covering can protect gas cans from internal condensation and heating, which can cause evaporation of gasoline. On coolers and lunch containers, the reflective foil slows ice melt and keeps food and drink fresh longer.

433

Pinpoint Pinholes

Pinholes and leaky seams in rain gear are an all-too-common problem. You can patch most of these leaks with a waterproof sealer, but first you have to find them.

Turn on a bright overhead light and hold the raingear up to it. Spots of light reveal the location of leaks.

434

Substitute Transducer Bracket

You may have trouble getting a suction cup bracket to stick on the transom of a rented or borrowed boat or you may break a permanently mounted transducer bracket while launching. Either way, you can't use the depth finder. But here's a solution.

Put the transducer in a small heavy-duty plastic bag filled with water. Seal the bag around the cord, then set the bag directly on the bottom of the boat (not on a false floor). You can also set the transducer in the bilge without the bag, making sure there's enough water in the bottom of the boat to keep the face of the transducer wet. As long as there is no air space between the transducer and the water, the unit reads through the hull, though signal strength and reception are reduced.

435

Store Line Cool and Out of Light

The best and least expensive way to buy fishing line is to buy bulk spools of the line tests you use. Be sure to store the line correctly to prevent damage. Sun and heat damage line and cause it to age prematurely. Store line in a dark and cool place. A basement is usually ideal. For the same reason, do not store tackle or line in the trunk of your car or in the glove compartment.

436

Bag Cold Feet

Cold feet are a big problem for ice fishermen. Perspiration condenses in your boots, dampening socks and wool liners and reducing their insulating value. Find a way to keep your socks and boot liners dry and your feet warm.

Trap moisture by slipping a bread bag over a light wool sock before putting on a heavy sock. Then put on your boot. Your inner sock gets damp, but the bag keeps your heavy sock and boot liner dry, so your foot doesn't get cold.

437

Personal Bug Deflectors

As you motor back toward the landing at dusk, you get pelted by insects. Unless you wear glasses, it's nearly impossible to keep the bugs out of your eyes. There's an easy solution to your problem, if you have a cap with a mesh crown support.

438

No-Hands Flashlight

Night fishing can be frustrating. You can't see well enough to tie knots, untangle backlashes, or unhook fish. Many of these jobs require two hands, so it's tough to hold a flashlight. But here's a way to see at night while keeping both hands free.

Strap a compact, battery-operated headlamp to your forehead. These lights, available in many sporting goods stores, are lightweight and you can aim them simply by turning your head.

Some headlamps come with two lights: a small one aimed downward for close-up work and a larger, brighter one for distance.

Headlamps also come in handy when gathering nightcrawlers. You can carry your worm container in one hand while grabbing the crawlers with the other.

439

Glue Rattle Sideways to Lip of Crankbaitt

Crankbaits often have rattles built into the lure, but you can add more noise and rattle sound with standard glass, plastic, and metal rattles available in all tackle shops. For the maximum sound, you must add the rattle sideways on the lure so the side-to-side action causes the beads in the rattle to bounce from one end to the other in the rattle container as the lure wobbles. Use epoxy cement to glue the rattle sideways to the lure at the junction of the body and the lip. That way, it will be out of the way of the line tie, stay on best with epoxy glue, and have maximum noise as the lure shakes from side to side on retrieve.

Pull the mesh down so it covers your eyes. The mesh is porous enough to see through, yet fine enough to stop bugs.

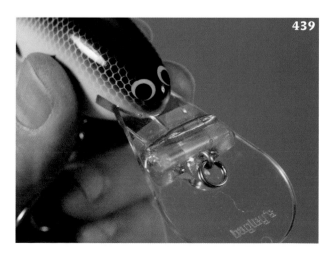

440

Reusable Hand Warmers

Chemical warmers keep hands and feet toasty in cold weather. They start heating as soon as you expose the contents to air. Though they produce heat for up to 12 hours, many outdoorsmen use them for only a couple hours and then throw them away, never realizing it's possible to stop the reaction and save the warmers for later. Here's how.

Seal the warmer in a small resealable plastic bag. The reaction requires oxygen, so it stops. As soon as you open the bag, the reaction starts up again.

441

Wader Wick

Once waders and hip boots get wet inside, they may take weeks to dry out. In the meantime, the cloth lining mildews or rots. And, of course, they're uncomfortable to use. Here's a way to dry them out quickly and you don't even have to hang them up.

Fold down the tops as far as you can to expose the lining to the air, then stuff loosely crumpled sheets of newspaper inside the boots. The paper wicks out moisture, which then evaporates. If the boots are very wet, replace the paper after a day.

442

Keep Lure Skirts from Sticking Together

Some plastic skirts stick together if exposed to heat or not used for a long time. To prevent this, sprinkle some cornstarch in with the skirts to keep them fresh and nonstick. When using the skirt, just shake off any excess cornstarch; the rest will come off the first time you throw the lure in the water.

443

Snagproof Anchor

If you fish over a bottom strewn with big rocks or manmade obstructions such as concrete slabs, you may hook your anchor so solidly you can't raise it. In fact, there may be nothing you can do but cut the rope. But there is a way you can fish over rocky bottoms without losing your anchor:

Use an anchor with soft lead flukes. If the anchor hangs up, cinch off the rope and run the motor. The snagged fluke straightens and the anchor pulls free. Pound the fluke back into place with a hammer.

444

Understand Your Blind Spot

It's a mistake to fish only where you "see" fish with your graph, LCR, or video. These devices detect bottom-hugging fish only if they're directly beneath the transducer. Elsewhere in the sound cone is a "blind spot" or "dead zone" just above the bottom. You won't see fish in this zone.

The dead zone is thickest at the edge of the cone and thinnest beneath the boat. The deeper the water and the wider the cone angle of your transducer, the thicker the blind spot.

You can't eliminate the blind spot, but you can gain a better understanding of what's happening beneath the boat by determining how thick the zone really is. Drop a jig to the bottom. Lower the rod tip to the water and reel in any slack. Lift the rod tip until the jig appears on your depth finder and note the distance between the water and rod tip. That distance between the water and rod tip, is the thickness of your blind spot in that particular part of the sound cone and depth of water.

445

Place Skirt in Front of Weedless Spoon

For more action and fish attraction in a weedless spoon, add a skirt to the line before tying on the spoon. Use the formed skirts that include a mounting hole for fitting onto lures since these are easiest to thread onto a line. It is also possible to use a latch hook tool or large needle threader to pull the line through the rubber "O" ring holding the skirt material in place. Then tie the line to the spoon and slide the skirt down to cover the front part of the spoon and to wiggle as the spoon wobbles on retrieve.

446

Bend Down Barbs for Kids

For safety and convenience, bend down all barbs on hooks when going on a fishing trip with kids. With bent-down barbs, it is easy to remove hooks from clothing, tackle, other gear, jackets, and even skin.

447

Secure Wood Bait Board

Surf fishermen, boat anglers, pier anglers, and jetty jockies are often preparing bait and using bait boards to cut, chop, dice, or fillet baits for fishing. To make this an easy task, use round head bolts, wide fender washers, and cap nuts (to prevent scratches) to secure a bait board to the top of a plastic fishing cooler. This cooler can be one in which you store bait, caught fish, or lunch. When drilling holes for the bait board and cooler, make sure the attaching nuts and bolts do not interfere with the lip and closure of the cooler lid.

448

Stay Dry in Big Waves

An anchored boat can be a wet place on a windy day, especially if your anchor rope is tethered to the highest point of your bow: the bow can't rise in big waves, so water splashes in.

The solution: tie the anchor rope to the bow eye, which is closer to the waterline. If you have an anchor winch on the bow, clip the rope to the bow eye. Any spring-loaded clip will work. Even with the clip in place, you can let out and take in rope with your anchor winch.

Now, with the anchor rope attached near the waterline, the boat will be able to rise and fall with the waves rather than to plunge bow first into each one.

449

Extend Battery Life

Many anglers charge their marine batteries with automatic battery chargers designed for automobiles. To provide a margin of safety against overcharging, many units shut off before they deliver a full charge. As a result, the battery discharges before it should. More important, repeated undercharging allows lead sulfate crystals to build up on the plates, reducing the battery's capacity and shortening its life. Here's how to tell if you're getting a full charge on your battery.

Charge the battery as usual. Wait 24 hours or turn on the boat's running lights for five minutes to get rid of "gas voltage" that causes a deceptively high reading right after charging. Then use a battery gauge to measure charge level.

If your automatic charger isn't fully charging your battery, use one with a timer or manual shut-off. By knowing the charge level, battery capacity, and charger output, you can use the information that came with your battery to calculate how long to leave the battery on your manual charger. Charging too long corrodes the plates, shortening battery life.

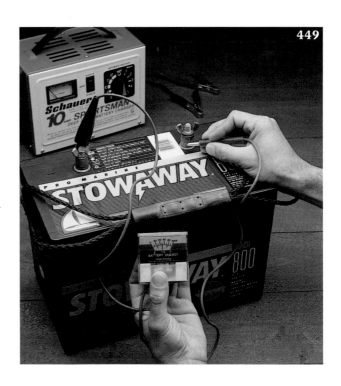

450

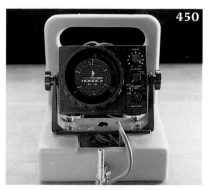

Get Better Readings through the Ice

When using a depth finder for ice fishing, you won't be able to see your lure and the fish below your hole unless the transducer points straight down. But it's hard to aim the transducer simply by eyeballing it. You need to get it lined up right every time.

451

Big "Hooks" Can Be Misleading

Many fishermen think a big hook on their paper graph, LCR, or video means a big fish. It could be, but it could also mean a small fish. Here's why.

Suppose two fish of equal size swim underneath your stationary boat. The first fish is only a few feet down, where the cone is narrow. As a result, it passes through the cone quickly and makes only a short mark. The second fish swims near the bottom, where the cone is wide. It spends more time in the cone and consequently makes a much longer mark.

Here's another example: You're drifting or slow-trolling and pass over a bluegill that is motionless or swimming slowly with the boat. It makes a long mark because it stays in the cone until the boat moves away. Then a good-sized bass swims rapidly through the cone. It makes a shorter mark because it passes through the cone more quickly.

Yet another possibility: You pass over two fish of identical size resting just off the bottom. The cone's edge passes over one, the center over the other. The fish in the center, where the cone is widest, stays in the cone longer and makes a bigger mark.

A more reliable indicator of fish size than arc length is arc thickness. The thickness depends on the strength of the reflected signal. And big fish reflect a much stronger signal than little fish.

Mount a surface, or "bull's-eye," level on the top of the transducer with silicone caulk. Before the caulk dries, make sure that the transducer is pointing straight down by placing the depth finder on the edge of a table (top), aiming the transducer at a hard floor, and adjusting it until you get the most intense signal. Then, with the transducer in the proper position, seat the level in the caulk (bottom) until the bubble is centered. When fishing, simply center the bubble to make sure the transducer is in the right position.

452

Avoid Depth Finder Interference

Some anglers run two or more depth finders simultaneously. But two units with transducers operating at similar frequencies interfere with each other.

If you plan to use two depth finders at the same time, make sure they have transducers with operating frequencies separated by at least 50 kilohertz. A flasher with a 192-kHz transducer, for instance, works fine with a 107-kHz LCR, but a 192-kHz and 200-kHz units are not compatible.

Be sure you're able to recognize interference.

Look for scattered red bands that spin around the dial on a flasher. Interference on a graph, LCR, or video appears as clutter.

453

Make Your Anchor Bite

When a strong wind blows, even a heavy anchor may drag across a sand or gravel bottom without digging in. A much heavier anchor might do the trick but would be a chore to use. You can make an ordinary anchor bite when you need it to.

454

Cold-Climate Boat Storage

If you store your boat in a cold climate, don't keep it in a level position. Water can puddle between the ribs and hull, inside gunwales, and in other small spaces, loosening or breaking parts of the boat as it freezes and expands. Even aluminum and fiberglass, materials normally considered weatherproof, can be damaged this way.

You can solve the problem by storing the boat with the bow raised slightly so water drains away. If you keep the boat right side up, remove the drain plug. Even if the boat is kept outside and exposed to rain and freezing temperatures, most water runs out before it can turn to ice.

455

Bump Rocks and Stumps with Lures

When fishing around structures, do not try to avoid stumps, standing timber, and rocks. A great tip for taking predatory gamefish is to run a lure into a stump, log, or rock and stop there to allow it to "die" at that spot. Wait a few seconds or longer. Then rapidly resume the retrieve, but be ready for a vicious strike.

456

Cushion Gas Cans

A gas can will vibrate as the motor runs and its metal edges will scuff the boat floor. As you fish and move around in the boat, the can rocks against the floor and makes noise. The photo shows a way to protect the floor and keep the can quiet.

1. Loop a small second anchor onto the rope, about 6 feet (1.8 m) above the main anchor.

2. Tighten the rope. The small anchor won't slide on the rope and you can easily take it off later.

3. Drop both anchors. The small one holds the rope down so the big one digs in. If you don't have a small anchor, use any heavy weight.

Slice a piece of garden hose lengthwise and slide it over the metal rim on the bottom of the gas can.

457

Cheaper Propane

Stoves and lanterns fueled by small propane cylinders are convenient for camping and fishing, but the cylinders are expensive and last only a few hours. There is a way you can substantially reduce the cost of the propane and avoid frequent trips to the store to buy replacement cylinders.

458

Make a River Drag Anchor

For small boat fishing in shallow rivers, make a river drag anchor for easier downstream drifting. Use a 3-foot (0.9 m) length of heavy chain, attached to a length of braided rope and a snap link in the other end of the rope. For easy results, make the total drag anchor no longer than the boat so you can run your engine without danger of tangling the anchor in the prop. If fishing deep waters, you can use the same drag anchor technique on a long rope, but you must bring in the anchor each time before running the engine.

459

Add Bottles of Ice to Cooler

An easy way to keep lunch and bait cool in a cooler is to not use crushed or cube ice, but to make your own ice containers. Save plastic bottles with their caps. They can be round or flat, large or small. Good possibilities are bottles sold for water, detergent soap, soft drinks, juices, etc. Wash each bottle thoroughly and then fill half full with water. Never completely fill, since the water expands as it becomes ice. Place the bottles upright in a freezer, allow to freeze, and then cap. They are ideal since they will not make sandwiches, caught fish, or snacks soggy as will crushed or cube ice.

460

Long-Lasting Trailer Lights

Leakage into trailer lights causes bulbs to burn out and corrosion in the sockets ruins the fixtures. If you have to replace your factory trailer lights, try the tip shown in the photo.

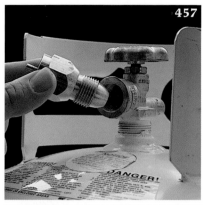

Refill a small cylinder from a large propane tank, using a brass coupler designed for that purpose. Pressure from the large tank forces the propane into the small tank with a hiss that sounds like air filling a tire. When the sound stops, the tank is full. Instructions come with the coupler; follow them for safety. By refilling cylinders, you pay only a tenth as much for the propane.

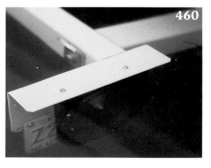

Install sealed, waterproof lights. If you can't find those made for boat trailers, you can use taillights designed for tractor-trailer rigs. Sealed lights are a little more expensive than non-waterproof lights, but they last much longer.

461

Bargain Wading Staff

A wading staff is a handy but pricey tool for stream fishermen.

Here's a way to make your own wading staff from a bamboo or fiberglass cross-country ski pole, which you can buy at closeout prices at the end of the ski season. Ski poles are strong and have a point that digs in for a good grip. A loop on the other end keeps the pole fastened to your wrist in case you stumble and makes a good place to tie a lanyard for clipping to your vest or belt.

But the circular basket on most ski poles hangs up in brush. You need a way to fix that problem.

462

Portable Anchor

Most anchors are too heavy to lug into hard-to-reach lakes and it's often difficult to find a rock with the right shape to tie a rope around. You can rig an anchor you can take anywhere.

463

Use Old Sock to Hold Spinning Spools

One easy way to store and carry spare reel spools for a spinning reel is to use an old sock. Usually you can store several spools in one sock. To do this, drop one spool in a sock and then fasten around the sock with a rubber band just above the spool. Then drop in a second and repeat until you have all the spools stored. You can also use a felt-tip marker to label each sock with a different reel model number or use one sock to store spools of several different reels used on one fishing trip.

464

Cheap "Power-Trim"

If your motor doesn't have power-trim or a shallow-water tilt mechanism, you've got a problem when running in shallow water. Here's a way to prevent grinding your prop into the bottom:

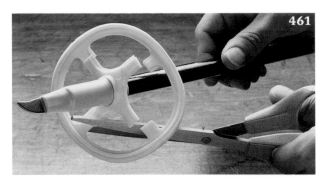

Trim back the plastic basket at the bottom of the pole so only 1-inch (2.5 cm) stubs remain. They keep the pole from sinking in a soft bottom, but won't catch on brush as easily as the full basket does.

Lower a mesh onion bag filled with rounded rocks and tied to your anchor rope. If you're fishing over a rocky bottom, put one bag inside another for extra strength. You can make an even more durable anchor bag from a basketball net. Cinch the bottom shut by running a short length of rope through the netting, place rocks inside, and cinch the top with the anchor rope.

Raise the outboard by hand, then lay a 2x2 (5x5 cm), an ax handle, or a piece of closet pole between the motor and the bracket that attaches it to the transom. Be sure the wood doesn't rest against and damage the reverse lock mechanism, a latch that prevents the motor from tilting up when you run it in reverse or neutral.

465

Scrub Tackle with Old Toothbrush

Save toothbrushes to use as scrubbing tools for
tackle. These are ideal for scrubbing around
crevices in reels, to remove grime from lures, and
to scrub around the guides of rods. Use a little
soap, scrub until clean, then rinse thoroughly.

466

PVC Tubes Make Good Surf Bags

Thin-wall (schedule 120) PVC tubing available
from hardware, plumbing, and household repair
stores can be used to make simple containers
for tin squids and other surf lures. For this, get
a small bag to be used as a surf bag on a belt or
in your beach buggy. Try to get a small squat bag
with square dimensions into which you can place
a series of cut tubes that hold tin squids, spoons,
and the like. An ideal bag might be 4 to 6 inches
(10 to 15 cm) deep, 10 to 12 inches (25 to 30
cm) wide and about 6 to 8 inches (15 to 20 cm)
high. Cut the tubing with a hacksaw to the height
of the bag and place side by side. If they fit snugly
in the bag, no additional work is necessary. If
they do not, then glue or tape the tubes into a
configuration that fits your bag. To use, just drop
the squids and metal lures into the bag, hook up
for easy grabbing and to prevent the hooks from
getting caught on the tube.

467

Use Worm Piece on Trailer Hook Eye

One easy way to hold a trailer hook in place is to
use a short scrap piece of plastic worm pushed
onto the hook eye, then the hook eye with worm
in place slid onto the main hook of the lure. This
is a typical system used for adding a second or
trailer hook to spinnerbaits and buzzbaits. It keeps
the hook in place for better hook-ups.

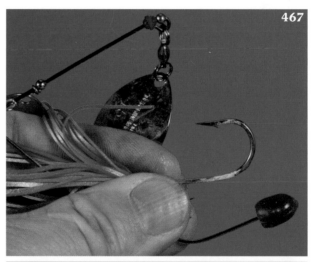

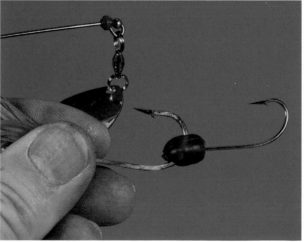

468

Camouflage Line with Felt-Tip Marker

You can camouflage your line by coloring it with a permanent felt tip marker. Use a wide felt-tip marker, coloring the line on the reel spool. Do not color the entire spool of line, but instead color just one side of the spool so the line will alternatively have the color of the manufactured line or the felt tip marker color. Several felt tip colors can be used if desired. To color line properly, mark the line with a felt tip, then make a short cast and color half of the line spool again. Repeat until all of the line necessary for a long cast is colored. To do this effectively, color the line when it is dry (BEFORE you fish) or by casting and coloring in the backyard. Any color felt tip can be used, with black, brown, blue, and green especially effective. Such colored lines are best when fishing weedy and slop-filled water or water with a lot of surface algae or kelp in both freshwater and saltwater areas.

469

The Lowdown on Motor Height

1. Check the height of the outboard's cavitation plate (arrow); it should be at about the same height as the bottom of the hull.

To get the best performance from your outboard, it must be set to the right height. If the shaft extends too far into the water, the extra drag reduces your speed, increases fuel consumption, and sprays water.

If the motor is too high, the hull interferes with the flow of water to the prop, causing it to over-rev and lose thrust. You need to determine if your motor is set to the proper height and what to do if it isn't.

470

Sharpen Hooks

The best way to sharpen hooks is by using a small file and working at an angle on both sides of the point. Once you have both angled sides sharp, finish with a final touch-up on the bottom of the point to make the point into a triangle when looked at from the end. Good tools for this include fine files and flat hones made for the purpose.

471

Add Bottles of Ice to Livewell

Make up bottles of ice by filling empty clean plastic bottles of ice with water, cap, freeze, and then add to your boat livewell to keep fish cool and in good condition. Do not completely fill the bottled with water to allow for ice expansion. You can reuse these bottles over and over to keep fish happy and livewell waters cool.

2. Elevate the motor if it's too low. Set a board on the transom as shown before putting on the motor and tightening the bracket. To elevate a motor that is bolted on, remove the bolts and reinsert them through holes lower in the bracket. If the motor is too high, lower it by reinserting the bolts in holes higher in the bracket; you may have to notch the transom to lower the motor.

472

Launching without a Ramp

Occasionally you may want to launch your boat where there's no concrete ramp or where low water has left several feet of soft sand between the ramp and the lake or river. If you try to back the boat in with your vehicle, you may get stuck.

473

Air Tank for Surf Fishing

Low tires are typically used when surf fishing to spread the tire footprint and to make it easier to drive on soft sand. Refilling tires before driving on hard highway surfaces is necessary to prevent tire wear and damage. If air hoses are not available, rig your beach or surf buggy with your own air tank available at most auto supply outfits. Make sure that you have the length of hose needed and the necessary tire valve fittings to fill your tires.

474

Wear Cleats for Saltwater Jetty Fishing

If fishing from a jetty, realize that all stone, concrete, and rubble jetties are slick with saltwater and algae. To prevent falls, make sure you use proper footwear. This usually means boots with cleats or felts that grip the rock to prevent falls.

1. Tie a strong rope from your trailer tongue to your hitch while the vehicle is parked on solid ground. Lower the tongue jack, if there is one. Then unhook the trailer, making sure it doesn't get away from you.

2. Roll the trailer and boat down to the water. In soft sand, you may have to push a bit. The rope should be short enough to keep the trailer from rolling all the way into the water. As you launch, stand on the trailer tongue for counterweight.

3. Haul the trailer slowly to solid ground while lifting the tongue enough to keep it from digging in. Don't attempt to roll the trailer out on the tongue jack, because the jack may catch on the ground and bend or break.

4. Load the boat after rolling the trailer back into the water with the rope attached. As you crank, you must stand on the trailer tongue to keep it from lifting. Hold the tongue up as the vehicle pulls the boat out.

475

Use Rubber Band for Loose Reel Seat

A reel that fits loosely on the reel seat can lead to loosened collet nuts which may cause the reel to fall off of the rod. Often this is caused by the reel seat having a loose or larger than normal hoods to hold what may be a slim or small reel foot on the reel. Here are two ways to correct this:

- Wrap a rubber band around the reel seat several times, spacing the wraps far apart to cover the full length of the seat. This will be flexible, yet fill up the space between the reel seat and the reel foot to prevent looseness and to allow tightening the reel in place.
- Use a length of rubber gasket material and glue a small rectangular strip to the reel seat where the reel foot sits. This will fill up the loose space so the reel fits tightly.

The rubber band is best for temporary use when only a small amount of looseness is observed. A gasket is best as a permanent solution and for looser reel situations.

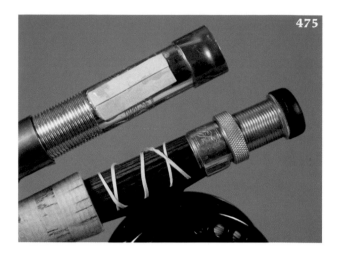

476

Don't Tire While Tubing

In a float tube, you can maintain your position in a breeze by kicking your feet, leaving your hands free to fish. But a stiff breeze can wear you out and if you let yourself drift, it may be a long way back to your put-in point. Here's a simple way of holding your position when you get tired of kicking.

Lower an anchor tied to a stout cord. Any weight will do, but a couple of pounds (1 kg) is all that's needed to hold a tube in a light wind. Tie the other end of the cord to the tube. Wrap the extra cord on a marker buoy or chunk of packing foam to keep it from tangling. When you drop anchor, simply half-hitch the line around the buoy and put it in a pocket of the tube. The anchor also lets you maintain your position over fish. Otherwise, it's easy to lose your bearings and drift away, even on a calm day.

477

Use Fishing Cap with Dark Under-Brim

Often the best fishing cap is a baseball style cap, but with a dark—preferably black—under-brim. The glare on the water causes light to bounce back into your eyes, particularly if you have a light-colored under-brim to direct that glare. To prevent this, buy a cap with a dark under-brim or use a black felt tip marker or black shoe polish to color the under-brim.

478

Easy Tie-Down for Cartop Loads

When carrying a canoe or small boat on a car, it's important to use a knot that can be tied and untied easily but holds the load securely. Many people throw the rope over the boat, tie a loop in the rope, run it under the rack and back through the loop, then pull the rope tight and tie it off. But when you want to use the rope again, you have a loop in it that's too tight to untie. A knot, called the trucker's hitch, gets the job done but won't leave a permanent loop in your rope.

479

Battery Safety

Batteries are filled with corrosive chemicals and produce explosive gases when charging. For these reasons, they are hazardous if used or charged improperly. Take these precautions to avoid trouble:

- Don't check the battery's charge, as some people do, by laying a wrench or other heavy piece of metal between the posts to make a spark. That tells you little about the charge level. But the surge of current through the wrench from a fully charged battery can melt lead posts in a fraction of a second, as the sparks can ignite accumulated hydrogen and oxygen, causing an explosion.
- To avoid sparks, connect the charger to the battery posts before plugging it in. When finished, unplug the charger before unhooking the leads. If the posts are dirty, they'll spark when you try to make the connection. Clean them with a wire brush first.
- Keep the vent caps on a standard battery when charging it. The caps are designed so flames from igniting gas can't follow back into the battery.
- If you spill battery acid, sprinkle on an equal volume of baking soda to neutralize it. Then add water to form a slurry, which you can clean up. Wear glasses and rubber gloves to protect eyes and hands.

1. Form a loop with two twists about a foot (30 cm) above the roof rack by slipping your fingers under the rope and rotating your wrist twice.

2. Draw the lower strand of the rope through the original loop, forming a second loop as shown. Pull the second loop tight.

3. Run the free end of the rope around the rack and then through the loop. Pull on the free end to tighten the rope over the load.

4. Wrap the free end around both strands of rope and tie a half-hitch, pulling it snug against the loop. Finish with a second half-hitch.

480

Canoe Rod Holders

Most canoes have no good place to lay a fishing rod. If you set them in the bottom, they slide to the center, where they can get broken. Here's a good way to keep rods where they're handy but out of the way:

481

Noise Reducer

Sheet foam is ideal for gluing to the bottom of a tackle box or other tackle containers to prevent scraping noise in a boat and to prevent the box from sliding around. Use contact cement to glue these foam sheets to the bottom of any box. This foam, in many colors, is available from craft stores.

482

Portable "Boat Winch"

If you want to pull your boat up on shore and leave it for awhile, you'll have to get it far enough out of the water that waves or wakes from passing boats can't pile over the transom. Lay two sections of 3-inch-diameter (7.6 cm) PVC pipe under your boat; roll the boat over them until it's high and dry.

483

Use Closet Rod for Poling Boat

Boat poling rods can run well over $1,000 for a 20- to 24-foot (6 to 7 m) graphite pole. Instead, consider using closet rods. These wood rods are available in 1¼- and 1½-inch (3 and 3.8 cm) diameters and lengths to 16 feet (4.8 m). Most home supply stores and lumberyards carry them. Be sure to choose one that is straight and straight-grained, the latter to prevent splinters. Before using the rod, sand with fine sandpaper and rub with linseed oil to preserve the pole. If desired, use a saw to cut a four-sided point on the end.

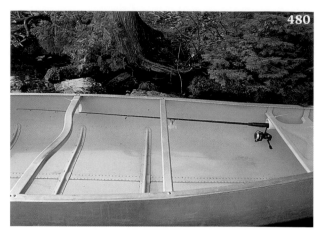

Slip the tip and handle of each rod into 2-inch-diameter (5 cm) pipe couplings attached to the cross-members and seats of the canoe with 6-inch-long (15 cm) nylon wire ties, available in hardware stores.

484

Temperature Probe

Electronic temperature probes measure the temperature from a thermocouple on the end of a cord and can register in either Celsius or Fahrenheit. They can take either air or water temperatures. It is also possible to leave the probe in the water to take constant water temperatures while fishing.

485

Pork Chunk Modification

There are many ways to modify pork chunks when fishing. These can be done when the pork chunk is a trailer to a lure such as a jig or spinnerbait or when fishing with the pork chunk alone. Also, use an awl or thin-blade knife to cut a small hole transversely through the body of the pork chunk. Use this hole to secure a plastic rattle for more noise.

486

Troll to Straighten Twisted Line

Line gets twisted when using lures that twist or when reeling spinning tackle when snagged or fighting a fish when you can't retrieve line. To correct this when boat fishing, remove all rigging, leaders, etc. from the tackle rigging so you have just the line on the reel. Then, while running your boat, allow a lot of line (100 to 200 feet [30 to 60 m]) out behind the boat and "troll" the line for at least several minutes. Longer is better.

487

Storing a Battery

If you store a boat battery improperly during the off-season, you may shorten its life or reduce its capacity. These tips keep a battery in good shape.

Disconnect the battery. Charge it fully and store it in a cool, dry place. Outside is fine, but be sure to keep it fully charged. Don't store a battery in a warm place; higher temperatures speed up the self-discharge reaction that causes lead sulfate crystals to form on the plates, ruining the battery. Contrary to popular belief, modern batteries can be stored on a cement floor without discharging.

Check the charge level every two months; never let it fall below 75 percent charge (12.4 volts). Subzero temperatures can freeze a discharged battery, almost always ruining it.

488

Use Two Hands for Longer Casts

To get the maximum distance out of any cast with spinning, spincast, or casting tackle, use both hands on the handle. Two hands give you more strength to punch out a cast, to put more force into the cast, and load the rod more for maximum distance. It is also easier on your wrist in a long day of fishing, allowing you to fish longer and more comfortably.

1. Taper the end of the chunk by cutting it with a knife so as to make it thinner and with less of a pork "shelf" between the chunk and leg parts.

2. Split part of the rear of the pork chunk, but do not invade the area with the hole for the hook. This gives the pork chunk more movement and leg action.

Walk the Plank

When launching a boat from a trailer with bunks, you may have to walk partway down the trailer frame to push the boat off. And to get it back on the trailer, you may have to walk on the frame once again, often in the dark. Trying to keep your balance is nearly impossible. Eventually you'll slip off and fall in the water and perhaps get seriously hurt. Here's something you can do to keep your footing.

490

PVC Rod Holders for Boats

Use 1½- or 2-inch (3.8 or 5 cm) schedule-40 PVC pipe to make horizontal rod holders along the gunwale of your boat. For this, fasten lengths of PVC pipe to the sides of the boat or to a board which in turn can be fastened to ribs and boat supports. Use these pipes as a sheath to hold tips of rods carried on board. For the rod handle, make a metal or wood rack to hold the rod handle and support the butt end of the rod. These create easy rod storage while also making it possible to unfasten the handle and pull the rod out of the sheath for instant use.

491

Use Long Gaff for Jetty Fishing

Jetties often place you far from the water's edge, making it difficult to land fish without special tools. One special tool that helps is a long-handled gaff. To make your own, fasten a large-diameter hook, barb filed off, to the end of a long length of 1-inch-diameter (2.5 cm) PVC pipe or a long length of aluminum tubing. PVC pipe is often the best, since you can also buy screw-on couplers to make the long handle jointed for easy travel and packing. Use the gaff as you would any gaff, hooking the fish and then pulling it to the top of the jetty hand over hand.

Stand on a lx8-inch (2.5 by 20.3 cm) plank that you've bolted to the trailer frame, while launching and loading your boat. Apply non-skid tape to the plank or paint it and sprinkle on sand before the paint dries to create a rough surface.

490

492

Charge Two Batteries at a Time

You come in after a day's fishing with two drained batteries and want to head out again first thing in the morning. How can you charge both with only one battery charger? You could charge one battery at a time, but you'd have to get up in the middle of the night to switch the cables. Instead, try this trick.

Connect the batteries in parallel (positive-to-positive, negative-to-negative) with 10-gauge or heavier cable. Hook the charger to one of the batteries. Use a trickle charger (also known as a taper-type), which includes most marine and automotive chargers. These gradually reduce the amount of current as the batteries approach full charge.

Multiple batteries take longer to charge than a single one. Two fully discharged batteries, for example, take about twice as long as a single fully discharged battery of equal size. For that reason, you'll need at least a 20-amp charger to do the job overnight. To make sure both batteries are fully charged, check each with a battery gauge or voltmeter.

Charging in parallel works even if batteries have been discharged to different levels. But if the difference is great, one battery reaches full charge long before the other and may overcharge while the other is still charging. In this situation, it's best to charge the batteries separately.

493

Avoid Alligators

Some electric trolling motors come equipped with alligator clips that connect to the battery terminals. The clips are quick and convenient. But with little surface area touching the terminals, alligator clips make a poor connection, causing a drop in voltage. To compensate, the trolling motor draws more current, draining the battery more quickly.

You need to improve the connection and get more running time out of your battery.

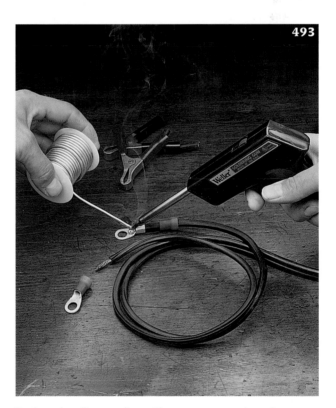

Replace the alligator clips with connectors, such as those shown, that can be attached snugly to the battery terminal with wing nuts. Connectors of this type provide plenty of surface area for the current to flow across. Crimp and then solder the connectors for the best conductivity. When installing any connector, be careful not to cut individual strands in the cable as you strip insulation. Losing even a few reduces conductivity and drains the battery faster.

Chapter 6
AFTER THE CATCH

It doesn't matter what species you catch, or how big it is. The pride of a successful outing brings its own special joy. Whether you keep the fish or release it, these tips will help you remember it.

PHOTOGRAPHING YOUR FISH

Good photos prolong the memory of a trip, but many folks have trouble taking interesting pictures. Their photos are out of focus or poorly lit, the background is cluttered; the fish looks stiff and lifeless. The problems are endless.

The first step toward taking better photos is to start with a reliable camera—either 35mm or digital. You may want one that is water-resistant or waterproof.

Serious photographers want interchangeable lenses. A zoom lens, about 28mm to 80mm, is an excellent choice because you can adjust it from wide-angle to low-power telephoto in an instant without the inconvenience of carrying extra lenses and changing them.

It pays to enroll in a course to learn the principles of photography and camera operation. Short courses are sometimes available at the store where you bought your camera or through community education programs. Perhaps the best way to improve your own photography is to study photographs you like and try to figure out why they appeal to you.

The tips that follow can help you take better pictures next time you go fishing. By paying attention to detail and giving up a few minutes of fishing to concentrate on your photography, you'll bring back better photographs.

Adjust for Bright Snow

Dazzling white backgrounds, such as new-fallen snow or big rapids, often fool photographers. For example, a picture of an ice fisherman on a sunny day is likely to be badly underexposed. The ice and snow will appear light gray, and the angler's face will be a dark shadow.

That happens because the camera's light meter reads and adjusts for the intense light of the background rather than the light coming off the subjects face. Here are two ways to remedy the problem.

If you're using a camera that can be operated in a manual mode, move close to your subject and set the exposure by metering off the person's face. Step back and take the photo. The angler's face will be properly exposed. The snow will be bright white and lack detail, but no one will care about that.

Some automatic cameras without a fully manual mode can be set to overexpose by up to two full stops, which will correct for snow or white water in the background. Some fully automatic cameras can be "fooled" by setting them to meter for a slower film. But many cameras read the film speed electronically off the film canister and can't be adjusted to compensate for these conditions.

495

Take Lots of Photos

If you're shooting with 35mm, don't spare the film. Compared to gas, tackle and other expenses, film is cheap. If you like the looks of a shot, take extras to compensate for those that are inevitably ruined by movement or awkward expressions. To make sure the exposure is correct, "bracket" your photos the way professional photographers do. For example, if you set your shutter speed at 1/250 second and your light meter says f8, try a second shot at f5.6, and a third at f11. That way you're sure one will have the proper exposure.

The top photo is exposed for snow, the bottom for the fisherman.

496

Low-Light Advantage

Shoot in the morning or evening, when the sun is low for the warmest, richest light. Good light makes a photo look vivid. The same shot at midday would have deep shadows and contrasting bright spots.

Midday glare presents another problem: the bright light can overpower all detail in a fish. Silvery fish such as trout and salmon are most likely to "burn out" by reflecting too much light. If you must shoot in bright light, turn the fish slightly until you get the best coloration and detail.

497

Play the Angles

Move higher or lower then your subject to make shots more interesting. Get below the level of the fish and shoot upward to emphasize the fish's size and eliminate boat clutter from a shot. On a stream, shoot down from a bank or bridge to get a good view of your friend as well as the surroundings.

498

There's More to Photos than Fish

There's more to fishing than fish, and there's more to fishing photographing your surroundings and the entire fishing experience. Little things like running the boat, changing lures and casting can make shots that are every bit as interesting as a picture of a trophy.

Harsh midday light casts dark shadows (inset); low light makes a subject come alive.

Wide-Angles Add Interest

A short, wide-angle lens (a 24mm or 28mm) makes objects in the fore-ground of your photo look bigger while shrinking objects in the background. As a result, a wide-angle image is often more interesting than a similar picture taken with a "normal" 50mm lens. Wide-angle lenses also let you keep both foreground and background objects in focus in the same photograph.

The same fish looks much bigger with a wide-angle lens (left) than with a normal lens (right).

500

Catch the Action

Try shooting action photos. Keep the camera loaded set for the prevailing light, and close at hand. Use a wide-angle lens to get the angler and the fish in the frame and in focus. Set the shutter speed at $\frac{1}{500}$ second to stop the action. With an auto-focus camera, remember to keep whatever you want in focus in the center of the frame.

501

Try Natural Poses

Try poses that don't look like poses. Do something with the fish. Have your partner pretend to land the fish, unhook it, lift it or release it. Photos like this have more life than the usual "meat" shot.

502

Fill the Frame

Turn your camera and take some "verticals" as well as the usual "horizontals." By matching your format to the shape of the subject, you can fill the frame with the fish and angler and eliminate dead space. The result: more interesting photos that have greater impact.

503

Fill Flash Fixes Flat Photos

If your subject is backlit, use "fill flash" to eliminate shadows and make your photo "pop."

Fill flash works best with a variable-power flash unit. With the camera in manual mode, set your shutter speed to synchronize with the flash, usually ¹⁄₆₀ second. Then set the aperture (f-stop) according to the cameras's light meter.

Adjust your flash unit according to the aperture setting of your camera and the distance to the subject. Then turn down the power dial by one f-stop. Otherwise the flash will "burn out" your subject. Shoot one or two shots. For insurance, lower your power setting by one more f- stops and shoots again.

You can't use fill flash with some fully automatic cameras because the flash won't fire in bright light. Other automatics have fill-flash buttons, so you can use the flash anytime.

504

Photograph Low-Water Lakes for Future Fishing

Take advantage of droughts on your fishing lakes and ponds that draw down the water level. Use these times to get out and photograph hot spots and locations that are normally covered by water. Key these photos to a map of the lake for an instant guide of where and how to fish after the water returns to normal levels. Digital still and video cameras make this an easy task.

A vertical fish fills the frame of a vertical shot (top) better than a horizontal (bottom).

505

Cheap Lens Protection

A polarizing filter, like polarized sungalses, cuts glare from the water and other objects. You adjust the filter for greater or less polarization. A filter also serves to protect the more expensive camera lens. A "skylight" or UV-haze filter gives protection without noticeably affecting the photo.

506

Taking Fishing Pictures in the Rain

To take photos in the rain using a standard film or digital SLR, carry along a standard plastic trash bag and a small roll of masking, duct, or painters tape. To protect the camera, cut or tear off a corner of the plastic bag to make a hole equivalent to the size of the camera lens. Place a lens shade on the lens. Then insert the camera into the bag with the lens shade sticking out of the hole. Tape the edge of the bag hole around the lens. Using this, you can stick your head in the bag to take photos without any damage to the camera. Just make sure the lens is pointed downward when not taking photos to avoid raindrops on the lens. Also, fold the open back of the bag over the camera body to protect it. If possible, use a zoom lens on the camera to maximize framing opportunities without changing the bag to another lens.

507

Homemade Waterproof Case for Small Cameras

A small point-and-shoot digital camera is ideal for field use and to take photos of your trips, friends, catches, and fishing adventures. Many of these are high quality with high-resolution megapixel screens and are small enough to fit into a shirt pocket. To protect your camera when fishing, keep it in a waterproof bag to prevent water damage. This is particularly important when wading while fishing trout streams and rivers. Good, inexpensive waterproof "cases" for these can be nothing more than a zipper-seal sandwich bag.

Glare from water (top) is reduced with a polarizing filter (bottom), which also protects the lens

TAKING CARE OF YOUR TROPHY

You've just brought the fish of a lifetime to boatside. This is the one you want for the wall. Be sure the things you do from here on out keep the fish in good condition so it looks as realistic on the wall as it does in the water.

If possible, land trophy muskies, pike, lake trout, and other big fish with a cradle, by hand, by carefully gaffing them in the mouth, or by beaching them. A landing net will knock off scales and split the tail and fins. Repairing is difficult.

Fish begin to decompose shortly after death, so freeze them as soon as you can. On trips where no freezer is available, keep the fish alive until you are ready to leave. Tether it on a 30-foot (9 m) nylon cord tied to its lower jaw. Attach the cord along a steep shoreline where the bottom is free of snags; this way, the fish can rest in deep, cool water.

508

Preparation

Take a color photograph of the fish while it is still alive. A photo will help your taxidermist restore the fish to its original color. Kill the fish by whacking it on the head with a blunt object. Don't use anything that would cut the skin or remove scales. Don't remove the entrails or gills.

In remote country, tether your fish in deep water to keep it alive.

Lead the fish into the cradle headfirst, then scoop it up. The mesh closes around the fish so it can't thrash. The fins and tail stay in good shape.

Avoid landing the fish with a net if you want to mount it. As the fish thrashes in the net, the tail and fins poke through the mesh and split.

Sprinkle powdered borax or a commercial color preservative on the fish's skin.

Wrap the fish in a wet towel, binding the fins tightly against the body to protect them. Don't fan the tail; doing so makes it easier to damage. Don't wrap the fish in newspaper; the ink discolors the skin.

Put the fish, still wrapped in the towel, in a large plastic bag. Squeeze out the air, wrap the bag with tape, then freeze. Label the bag with your name, address, fishing license number, and date the fish was caught. This information will aid any conservation officer that checks your catch. It will also help your taxidermist identify the fish as yours.

If possible, store the fish in a chest freezer, which keeps items colder than freezer-refrigerator combinations. Avoid frost-free freezers, which rely on a small fan to circulate air to prevent frost build-up. The circulation can dry out the fish and contribute to freezer burn.

If a mount you admire was done by a taxidermy company, get the name of the person who did the work. Some companies employ many taxidermists and all are not equally skilled.

More and more anglers release their trophies and buy "museum mount" fiberglass or carbon-fiber replicas of their catches. To get the best likeness of your fish, carefully measure its length and girth. Weigh it if you have a scale. Finally, take a color photo to help match the model to the original.

509

Caring for Your Mount

When finding a place on your wall for your trophy, avoid heat and humidity. A fish may look great over the fireplace, but the heat dries it out. Also, direct sunlight may cause the fish to fade.

Dust your mount occasionally with a feather-duster or a soft cloth dampened with water. Gently stroke the fish from the head toward the tail to avoid damaging any of the scales.

Measure length and girth to order a proper-sized reproduction.

Sprinkle color preservative on the fish before wrapping it in a wet towel to protect the skin, and tail.

Color preservative was used on the half toward the head for demonstration purposes; the area toward the tail wasn't treated.

CERTIFYING A RECORD

If you catch a fish you think may qualify as a record you'll have to follow several procedures to get it certified. The following information is based on the requirements of the IGFA (International Game Fish Association), the major international record-keeping organization. These procedures will also satisfy the state-record requirements of most conservation agencies.

Should you hook a potential record, don't let anyone touch your line or rod or help you land the fish. Any assistance will disqualify the catch, with this exception: someone else may net or gaff the fish.

Measure fork length from the tip of the lower jaw (or the upper jaw if that sticks out farther) to the fork of the tail. Measure total length from the tip of the jaw to the end of the tail. Measure girth around the largest circumference.

510

Step-by-Step

Weigh the fish as soon as possible on a scale checked and certified for accuracy by a government agency or accredited commercial organization. These scales may be found in sporting goods stores, grocery stores and butcher shops. The scales should bear a stamp with a number, date of inspection, and name of inspector. Record this information. If the scale available is not certified, weigh the fish anyway. The scale can be verified for accuracy later, and the weight of the fish adjusted, if necessary.

Weigh the fish only once in the presence of two witnesses. Record their names and addresses. You cannot be a witness to your own application.

Measure the fish's girth and length.

Photograph everything. Take photos of the fish lying on a flat surface to aid in determining what species it is. If you have a ruler, lay it next to the fish. Photograph the fish hanging vertically. Take photos of the angler with the fish. Photograph the tackle used to land it. Also take a picture of the fish on the scale with the weight clearly visible. These photos must accompany your application.

A professional taxonomist or fisheries biologist must examine the fish if it's a potential all-tackle record, if you think it's a hybrid, or if for any reason the identification of the species will be in doubt from a photo alone. In these instances, the biologist must attest to the identification in writing.

Don't cut the fish open; this raises suspicions that weight may have been added to the fish and later removed. The record-keeping agency may ask that the fish be opened to verify no weight was added.

If you are applying for a line-class record, clip a line sample to send in with your application. Save the first 50 feet of line from a spinning or baitcasting outfit. For a fly-fishing record, the IGFA requires the fly, entire leader, and 1 inch of fly line, all knots intact. Wrap the line on notched cardboard. The sample will be laboratory tested for strength.

This is only a partial list of requirements. If you think you have a world or line-class record, consult the IGFA for more details, by visiting their website at www.igfa.org.

The IGFA requires that your application be filled out and returned within 60 days of catching the fish.

CARE & PREPARATION OF FISH

Most anglers don't take trophy fish very often. If they don't release the fish, they want to make a shore lunch of it or take it home for eating later with the family. Here are a few tips to help get your catch to the table.

511

Super-Chilling Fish

It's hard to keep fish fresh on long trips into the back-country. You'll be lucky to keep them more than two or three days on ordinary ice. But you can keep them for a full week by "super-chilling" them with a mixture of ice and salt. Because the ice-salt combination has a lower melting point, about 28°F (-2°C), the fish stay colder.

You can super-chill fillets, steaks or whole fish that have been gutted and gilled. Wrap the fish in aluminum foil or plastic cling wrap. Add 1 pound (0.45 kg)of coarse ice-cream salt to 20 (9 kg) pounds of crushed ice and stir thoroughly. If you need less of the salt-ice mixture, reduce the ingredients proportionally.

Place the wrapped fish on a 4-inch (10 cm) bed of the salt-ice. Add alternating layers of fish and salt-ice, finishing with a generous topping of the salt-ice mixture. As the ice melts, drain the cooler and add more of the salt-ice.

512

"Butterfly" Your Fish

Butterflying is a fast way to prepare an appetizing cut from a large smooth-skinned fish, such as salmon, large trout, and catfish. It also works well with some saltwater fish, such as wahoo and tuna.

You can butterfly fillets quickly, and you don't dull your knife. The finished cut is easier to eat than a steak because it has no bones. And it's more appealing because the flesh is on the outside; the inedible skin and fat are tucked away on the inside.

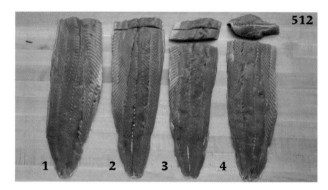

Cut a (1) fillet from the fish. Remove the rib bones, but don't skin the fillet. (2) Slice across the fillet, about an inch from the end, cutting through the meat but not the skin. (3) Make a second cut, parallel to the first and about an inch (2.5 cm) farther from the end; slice completely through both the meat and the skin. (4) Fold the piece of fish backwards along the first cut so the meat is on the outside and the skin is on the inside. Butterfly the rest of the fillet, except the tail section.

513

Freeze Fish Longer

Most anglers freeze much of the fish they catch. But fish loses its fresh taste after a while in the freezer. Lean fish, such as walleyes, will keep well for three to four months. Oily fish, such as salmon or trout, will begin to develop a strong, fishy taste in only about half of that time.

Here's a trick to extend freezer life by several months. Soak the fish for 20 seconds in lemon juice or a solution of 2 tablespoons (30 ml) of ascorbic acid (available in drugstores) in 1 quart (1 liter) of water. The ascorbic acid, which is also present in lemon juice, retards spoilage by counteracting oxidation and slowing the growth of microorganisms. After soaking, double-wrap the fish and freeze it immediately.

514

Freshwater "Scallops"

Many anglers cut fillets off walleyes and discard the rest. They don't realize they're throwing away some of the best meat—the cheeks. They have a taste and texture very much like scallops. But cheeks of even a good-sized walleye are tough to skin because they don't give you much to hold onto. Here's a trick that makes the job quicker and easier.

1. Cut under the cheek, leaving the cheek connected to the fish by a small flap of skin just behind the eye.

2. Skin the cheek meat by peeling it off with your thumb and forefinger.

515

Breakable Fish Bricks

Resealable plastic bags come in handy for freezing fish. Simply drop the fish in the bag, fill the bag with water, seal it and freeze it. The fish will stay fresh for months. But the bags freeze in irregular shapes that don't stack well in the freezer. And you have to thaw out the entire bag to use a small portion.

Here's a way to freeze fish in plastic bags so the packages stack neatly, and the contents are easy to identify. Best of all, individual pieces of fish can be removed so you don't have to thaw the whole package.

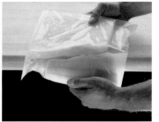

1. Cover whole fish or fillets with water as they lie side-by-side in a resealable bag in a cake pan. Leave a little space between them. Squeeze out the air, and seal the bag. Prepare several bags of fish, laying them in the pan in layers. Put the pan in the freezer. When the fish is frozen, remove the bags from the pan and stack them in the freezer.

2. Break off as many pieces of fish as you need for a meal by pushing the bag against the edge of a countertop. Don't rip the plastic. Remove the broken-off portion, reseal the bag and return it to the freezer.

516

No Bones About It

The fillets of many kinds of fish contain a row of small bones, called epipleural ribs, that lie right above the rib cage. There is an easy way to get rid of these bones.

517

No More Awful Offal

If you clean fish on Sunday, but your garbage collector doesn't come till Wednesday, the carcasses will have a long time to ripen and smell. Prevent the problem by sealing the fish remains in a plastic bag and freezing them solid. Set them out, still frozen, on the day of garbage pickup.

Remove the row of bones after first locating it with your finger. Slice through the fillet along one side of the bones for the length of the body cavity. Then slice along the other side, forming a thin strip that you can lift out to leave a completely boneless fillet.

518

Five-Piece Y-Bone Method

Members of the pike family have delicious, flaky meat. But the Y-Bones are bothersome enough that some people refuse to eat these fish.

Although there are a couple of ways to remove these bones, most fishermen don't know, so they have to pick them out at the table.

Here's one easy way to make boneless fillets from pike and pickerel. Then you can forget about Y-bones and enjoy your meal.

519

Get Rid of Muddy Taste

Some fish, such as bass and catfish, pick up a weedy or muddy taste from the water they live in. You can get rid of most of this taste:

1. Soak the pieces of fish for approximately 30 minutes in a mixture of a quart of water and ½ teaspoon (2.5 ml) of baking soda. After soaking, rinse the fish with water.
2. Or, soak the fish for an hour in fresh, cold whole milk. Then rinse the fish with water. Many of the molecules that cause the disagreeable flavor bind to the proteins in the milk and wash away.

520

Reduce Contaminants

Many waters contain pollutants that concentrate in fish flesh. You can reduce your consumption of harmful chemicals by eating small fish of a given species. Small fish have had less time to accumulate pollutants. Predator fish usually have the most contaminants. They're highest on the food chain, so they concentrate the chemicals found in the smaller fish they eat.

Many contaminants—including PCBs, dioxin, and DDT—are soluble in oil, so fatty fish like trout and salmon have a higher contaminant level than lean fish like walleyes and pike.

1. Cut down behind the head. Turn the blade toward the tail and run it along the backbone. Slice upward just ahead of the dorsal fin, cutting away the back fillet.

2. Loosen the skin along each edge of the back fillet so it will lie flat on the cutting surface. Now you can skin the fillet as you would any other.

3. Remove the side of the fillets by first cutting down to the backbone, once behind the head, and a second time ahead of the dorsal fin. Feel along the back to find the Y-bones. With the fish on its side, insert your knife just above the Y-bones and cut away a fillet so the Y-bones remain attached to the fish. Remove the fillet from the other side in the same way. Skin the fillets.

4. Cut off the fillets from each side of the tail section by slicing along the backbone. There are no Y-bones in this part of the fish. Skin the tail fillets. You now have five boneless fillets.

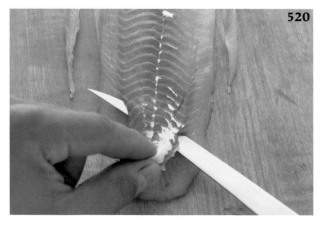

Cut away the fatty tissue found along the lateral line, back and belly, to minimize oil-soluble contaminants.

TIP CONTRIBUTORS

All tips by C. Boyd Pfeiffer, except the following:

7	Larry Ehardt, South Fork, CO
8	Jim Keuten, Duluth, MN
10	Larry Bollig, Ham Lake, MN
13	TL Hegeholz, Holcombe, WI
18	Rod Sather, Devils Lake, ND
25	David Marquardt, Forest Lake, MN
34	Bill Murphy, El Cajon, CA
38	Ray Mertes, Trempealeau, WI
44	Steve Rajeff, Suquamish, WA
45	Larry Bollig
46	George Huber, Etlan, VA
48	Jim Keuten
50	Guido Hibdon, Gravois Hills, MO
64	Dave Diffely, Parshall, ND
66	Timothy Maxey, Concord, VA
74	Bill Cork, Plano, IL
80	John Herrick, Ely, MN
90	Steve Grooms
91	Steve Grooms
96	Steve Grooms
99	Larry Bollig
100	Ronnie Kovach, Huntington Beach, CA
108	Steve Lindberg, Woodbury, MN
112	Skip Adams, Sebring, FL
114	Frankie Dusenka, Chisago City, MN
115	Mike Mladenik, Crivitz, WI
117	Don Brauer, Fort Lauderdale, FL
119	Woo Daves, Chester, VA
121	Bill Murphy
122	Colin Stass, Blenheim, Ontario
123	Kurt Johnson, Plymouth, MN
131	Kurt Johnson
132	Kent Oderman, Parshall, ND
134	Shaw E. Grigsby, Jr., Gainesville, FL
135	Dick Garlock
136	Joe Bucher
138	Dick Grzywinski, St. Paul, MN
142	Jim Keuten
149	Jim Keuten
148	Joe Bucher, Boulder Junction, WI
150	Tom Neustrom
152	David H. Ohrtman, Chisago City, MN
162	Mark Windels, Crookston, MN
164	Joe Bucher
165	George Sandell, Eden Prairie, MN
166	Joe Bucher, Mark Windels
167	Joe Bucher
168	Joe Bucher
170	Tom Gelb, Milwaukee, WI
171	Joe Bucher

172	Joe Bucher
174	Mark Windels
175	Don Scott, Allegan, MI
178	Joe Bucher; John Kuhn, Kona, HI
179	Don Pursch
180	Mark Emery
181	J.R. Humphrey, St. Paul, MN
182	Jim Keuten
183	Al Troth, Dillon, MT
184	Craig Woods, Dorset, VT
186	Tom Helgeson, Minneapolis, MN
187	Jim Keuten
190	John Crawford, Lewiston, ID
191	Al Troth
193	Bob Nicholson, Baldwin, MI
194	Jim Keuten
195	Bob Nicholson
198	Kevin D. Becker, Plymouth, MN
199	Capt. John Olson, New Berlin, WI
203	Shawn Perich, Grand Marais, MN
204	Jim Keuten
205	Jim Keuten
207	Larry Bollig
208	Chuck Thompson, Mt. Prospect, IL
209	Joe Bucher
210	Eddie Slater, Indianola, MS
212	Dennis Hunt, St. Paul, MN
214	Dave Genz, Jon Poehler
215	Dave Genz, Spring Lake Park, MN
216	Dick Gasaway, Littleton, CO
218	Dan Goihl, Melrose, MN; Jon Poehler
220	Dick Grzywinski
221	Bill Hammer, Lake City, MN
222	Dick Grzywinski
223	Gary Clancy; Joel Vance, Jefferson City, MO
225	Doug Stange, Brainerd, MN
227	Gary Clancy, Byron, MN
228	Steve Payne, Post Falls, ID
229	Eduard L. Telders
232	Jim Schneider, New Ulm, MN
233	Jim Schneider
234	Eduard L. Telders, Renton, WA
235	Jim McDonald, Royal, IA
236	Doug Stange
238	John Sellers, Cross, SC
239	Gary Clancy
297	Mark Emery
298	Mark Emery
307	Hank Gibson, Keswick, Ontario
311	Don Iovino

324	Joe Bucher
327	Mark Emery
340	T.L. Hegeholz
341	John Storm, Norman, OK
343	Joe Bucher
348	J. R. Humphrey
362	Ronnie Kovach
365	Dale Odom, Pittsburgh, IL
368	Charles Westby, Belize City, Belize
372	Tom Pfister, Duluth, MN
374	Steve Murray, Clear Lake, IA
375	Tony Thompson, Pearl, MS
376	Robert C. Hanna, Hillsdale, MI
378	Michael D. Mills, Warren, OH
379	Butch Furtman, Duluth, MN
383	Bruce Holt, Woodland, WA
386	Robert Traczyk, Hurley, WI
387	Gregg Thorne
388	Capt. Butch LoSasso, Kona, HI
389	Tom Neustrom
392	Cliff Jacobson, Hastings, MN
394	Steve Crawford, Eustis, FL
395	Bruce Holt
398	Bob Ponds, Brandon, MS
399	Gene Schmidt, Shell Knob, MO
408	Gregg Thorne, Fridley, MN
409	Bob Sonenstahl, Wayzata, MN
410	Buck Baxter, Boise, ID; Ronnie Kovach
412	George Collins, Charleston Heights, SC
416	Tom Neustrom
418	Mark Emery
419	Gregg Thorne
424	T.L. Hegeholz
433	Cliff Jacobson
434	Joe Bucher
437	Mark Emery
443	Dan Makowsky, Duluth, MN
444	Larry Bollig
450	Dave Genz
451	Larry Bollig
454	Greg Harvey, Marathon, NY
457	Jon Poehler
460	Steve Crawford
461	J.R. Humphrey
462	Jack Gosler, Utica, MI; Cliff Jacobson
476	Tom Anderson, Fridley, MN
508	Don Berger, Forest Lake, MN; Steve Crawford
513	Billy Joe Cross, Jackson, MS
517	Billy Joe Cross

INDEX

Creative Publishing international
Your Complete Source of How-to Information for the Outdoors

Hunting Books
- Advanced Turkey Hunting
- Advanced Whitetail Hunting
- Beginner's Guide to Birdwatching
- Black Bear Hunting
- Bowhunting Equipment & Skills
- Bowhunter's Guide to Accurate Shooting
- The Complete Guide to Hunting
- Dog Training
- How to Think Like a Survivor
- Hunting Record-Book Bucks
- Mule Deer Hunting
- Outdoor Guide to Using Your GPS
- Ultimate Elk Hunting
- Waterfowl Hunting
- Whitetail Addicts Manual
- Whitetail Hunting
- Whitetail Techniques & Tactics

Fishing Books
- Advanced Bass Fishing
- The Art of Freshwater Fishing
- The Complete Guide to Freshwater Fishing

- Fishing for Catfish
- Fishing Tips & Tricks
- Fishing with Artificial Lures
- Inshore Salt Water Fishing
- Kids Gone Campin'
- Kids Gone Fishin'
- Kids Gone Paddlin'
- Largemouth Bass
- Live Bait Fishing
- Modern Methods of Ice Fishing
- Northern Pike & Muskie
- Catching Panfish
- Salt Water Fishing Tactics
- Smallmouth Bass
- Striped Bass Fishing: Salt Water Strategies
- Successful Walleye Fishing
- Trout
- Ultralight Fishing

Fly Fishing Books
- The Art of Fly Tying + CD-ROM
- Complete Photo Guide to Fly Fishing
- Complete Photo Guide to Fly Tying

- Fishing Dry Flies
- Fly-Fishing Equipment & Skills
- Fly Fishing for Beginners
- Fly Fishing for Trout in Streams
- Fly-Tying Techniques & Patterns

Cookbooks
- All-Time Favorite Game Bird Recipes
- America's Favorite Fish Recipes
- America's Favorite Wild Game Recipes
- Backyard Grilling
- Cooking Wild in Kate's Kitchen
- Dressing & Cooking Wild Game
- The New Cleaning & Cooking Fish
- Preparing Fish & Wild Game
- The Saltwater Cookbook
- Venison Cookery
- The Wild Butcher
- The Wild Fish Cookbook
- The Wild Game Cookbook

To purchase these or other Creative Publishing international titles, contact your local bookseller, or visit our website at
www.creativepub.com

The Complete
FLY FISHERMAN™